HOW CUSTOMERS BEHAVE:
TURNING MARKETING COMPLEXITY
INTO STRATEGIC ADVANTAGE

by

Greg Silverman

Dejan Duzevik

Andrea Jones-Rooy

Silverman, Greg
How Customers Behave: Turning Marketing Complexity into
Strategic Advantage

ISBN: 978-0-61553244-8

TABLE OF CONTENTS

INTRODUCTION

We wrote this book to draw attention to a decade of effort that has been put into the development of a set of ideas that once was a product and is now a business.

The ideas originate from far-ranging fields that represent an intellectual quest for improvement and difference-making in the Marketing Analytics field. The product is a software platform that allows users to simulate complex environments (like a market) that are filled with changing agents (people) as they influence each other (via social networks), and are influenced by external forces (advertising and media) about the options they choose from (products and services).

The software allows marketing executives to simulate the market environment in which they, their customers, their competition, and their products all operate. It uses an analytical technique called "Agent-Based Modeling" (ABM), which simulates individual behavior within a changing environment to uncover the causes of aggregate, nonlinear and often surprising outcomes. In the marketing case, the core unit of analysis is the customer, and one can change features of the environment, the product, message, timing, and spending allocation in order to see the effects on sales, brand equity, awareness and word-of-mouth (WOM).

Above all, an ABM is an aggregator of data, methodologies, and science. An ABM works with qualitative or quantitative data. It can also operate with assumptions made in the absence of data using expert insight or the wisdom of crowds. Companies that use ABM combine their various and disparate data with insight and judgment in a common framework.

This is possible since the core of the ABM functionality comes from a handful of relatively simple rules of individual agents. The most important factors in a consumer ABM are the probabilities with which people do certain behaviors (e.g., decide which product to buy or talk to another person) and the properties of the people (e.g., perceptions, awareness, or purchase drivers). Whether we have terabytes of data, focus group results, or a single domain expert, an ABM can produce meaningful and useful results. In addition, the ABM becomes a data repository: market research, brand trackers, segmentation studies, media spending, and product specifications coexist as foundations of the individual rules of the ABM.

Similar to its role as a data aggregator, an ABM can integrate various methodologies. Econometric research in the form of response curves can feed into the ABM to determine the relative power of different media channels. A Monte Carlo analysis, running the same model over and over again to have a probabilistic set of outcomes rather than one answer, goes hand-in-hand with probabilistic ABMs.

The simulated mind of a consumer may take the form of a set of differential equations. Various forms of optimizers can be introduced into an ABM for calibration, maximization of goals, or sensitivity analysis. And, finally, the behavioral probabilities of the individual agents may change using Bayesian economics as new data becomes available to the ABM.

While the aggregation of data is useful from a practical and organizational standpoint, the aggregation of methodologies allows us to augment existing approaches into a holistic simulation. The real power of ABMs comes from the ability to unify vastly different, and often isolated, scientific approaches into a common analytical framework. Four questions regarding Community, Coordination, Choice, and Chance, each tied to sciences dedicated specifically to these topics, are the intellectual foundation that is the base of a new means for accurate forecasting of social dynamics in the marketing environment.

Community: How do social networks work? Network science analyzes the mathematics of product adoption and the spread of ideas.

Coordination: How do people influence each other? Sociology and psychology propose a handful of mechanisms behind social influence, conformity, persuasion, and trust, all playing a role in converging people who have never even met to a set of common behaviors and similar responses to similar stimuli.

Choice: How do people make decisions? Behavioral economists have uncovered myriad heuristics and biases that show that people actually make choices that deviate from what traditional economic models prescribe. In addition, cognitive scientists have made great strides toward replicating the decision-making of real people through artificial intelligence, while neuroscientists are slowly uncovering the effects of minute interactions of millions of synapses on the formation of opinions, tastes, and knowledge.

Chance: How can we predict anything that is as highly dependent on underlying and unobservable probabilities as human behavior is? Quantum mechanics is the most accurate description of the universe, with application to such quotidian objects as transistors, GPSs, and lasers, all the while being based on a theory that postulates that some properties of the system will never be known, and that every event, no matter how elementary, can only be understood as a probability. Combining those probabilities into a unified platform for analysis led us to agent-based modeling.

Many people have never heard of ABMs, even though it is a growing field. Many who have already heard about it may not know very much about it. And the vast majority of people have never built an agent-based model, much less conducted analyses with them. We hope this book changes that.

PART 1

INTERCONNECTED MODELS OF THE WORLD:

THE MIND, NETWORKS, AND

PRINCIPLES OF AGENT-BASED MODELING

The Customer Journey

All people wake up needing things, and go about their day trying to fill those needs. We call this daily process the customer journey. People take journeys each day, each week, each year, and over a lifetime. They are nested journeys.

Marketing affects all of our views in terms of how the journey works, as well as how products may or may not satisfy our needs. Marketing can also affect the very needs we think we have (e.g., I'll work out if I buy that treadmill).

In this chapter we introduce a new approach to marketing and to human decision making (and human behavior — not quite the same thing) that incorporates science about the individual, the network, and what we know about how marketing affects people's views. Then we layer on top of these foundations a philosophy of science and the world called agent-based modeling. If this talk about layering and enriching has you thinking about cakes, that's great, with a cherry on top.

AN EXAMPLE JOURNEY

You are about to make a choice that carries profound consequences. What you do in the next few minutes will affect everything from your most personal relationships, to the many different people who make up your friendship circles — even perfect strangers. It will have consequences for your health, your financial future, and your overall peace of mind. It impacts the environment. It affects, quite possibly, the fate of the very world as we know it.

This is only a slight exaggeration. You are about to buy a birthday cake for your significant other. And right now, you're in the tensest moment of all: placing your order. You've been preparing for this moment. Over the weekend, you researched online for the best bakeries in town. You called up your friend Allen who is always in the know. Your co-workers chimed in at the coffee machine. You took off work early to get all the way downtown, satisfied with your choice of bakery, and fully ready to get your significant other's favorite: Death by Chocolate.

On your way in from your parked car to the bakery, you pass a woman eating a white cupcake with yellow frosting. It strikes you as rather elegant. Now you're questioning your conviction about the chocolate. Then you remember your colleague suggested you make a cake rather than buy one — it's more personal. Now you're really wavering. Should you go buy a vanilla cake mix or stay here and buy a pre-made chocolate cake?

If you hadn't passed the woman, you wouldn't be rethinking your chocolate choice. If you hadn't spoken with Allen, you wouldn't have chosen this bakery. If you hadn't interacted with those particular coworkers, you wouldn't suddenly be thinking you should leave this perfectly nice bakery and go buy a mix from the grocery store.

These sorts of processes take place every day. Small, happenstance events can lead to real behavioral changes. In the aggregate, sometimes they are a wash. Other times, however, they spiral up or down, leading to big events, unplanned turns, and success or failure in broad strokes.

The focus of agent-based modeling is understanding how interactions work, when they happen, and to what outcomes they give rise. These things can be anything from people to advertisements to conversations to the products we use.

If you are reading this book, it's likely you are in the field of marketing. For marketers, the most important interactions are those that take place between customers, marketers, and the product. In agent-based modeling, people who are not purchasing but are part of the process (significant others, friends, doctors, etc.) also influence the results, even if they don't make purchases themselves. Interactions have long been very challenging to study rigorously. People are already hard to understand as individuals much less in pairs or groups.

When it comes to individuals, fields like cognitive science, behavioral economics, and psychology help get us a long way. We could write a list of characteristics of one person and a list about another person and consider what they might do on their own. Things get a lot more difficult to predict when we set these two people up to interact. What will happen? Who will influence whom? Will they get along? Will they learn something? When they meet a third person after this, what influence will they carry over to their new conversation?

What happens when each of those people meet fifty others? We all interact with many people every day. How interactions change behavior and cause ideas to spread and evolve becomes very complex very fast. Social interactions are kind of like a giant echoing, multidimensional game of Telephone. In recent decades, however, conceptual and technological advancements have allowed us to study interaction much more carefully and comprehensively than ever before.

Before we continue, there are two more important concepts: information and proactivity. As a marketer, you are interested in the flow of information. The most obvious information transaction about which you care is how messages travel between customers. But you also want information to flow between your company and your customers, as well as between employees within your own company, such as between operations and customer service. You also want information to flow between you and your competitors. How else will you really know what they're up to, and how you can respond? As will become clear over the course of this book, information flows — in the form of feedback — are crucial to being intelligent, inquisitive, and ready when it comes to beating competitors and delivering to people what they want.

Fast and accurate feedback is key to becoming proactive, rather than simply reactive. Being proactive means not only acting first, but also acting with confidence bolstered by your analyses. By the end of the book, you will develop with us a model that is forward thinking, not just summaries of past performance.

WHERE WE GO FROM HERE

What of the cake situation from above? It turns out, you decided to be old-fashioned and bake a cake for your significant other. You skip out of the fancy bakery, pop into the grocery store, and pick up a cheerful box with a big yellow cake on the front.

That evening, as you apply frosting to the cake in your bright, little kitchen, you're glad. The cake's warm scent reminds you of your childhood. Your thoughts turn to your significant other and friends. Your life is a little like this cake — a small, simple thing. Just sweet enough. Just sunny yellow enough. And just unpolished, asymmetric, and lumpy enough (you're no master chef here) to be just right.

Perfect enough to tell your friends about it? Who knows? Actually, you do know. You've known all along but have not had the vocabulary or tools to study it directly.

COMPONENTS OF THE CUSTOMER JOURNEY

The customer journey has three major parts: The first is the customer, or as we'll come to call him/her, the "agent." Agent is a great word for the customer because, in addition to it being a standard term elsewhere in the agent-based modeling literature, it is close to the word "agency," which is what we assume all customers have in a simulation. Goal-seeking, imperfectly informed, boundedly rational people are what make up our customer base. They have needs they wish to fill, and our job is to figure out how to fill them — or point them out.

Specifically, we care about the mind of the customer, or agent, and all the feelings and thoughts to which it gives rise. In the next chapter we consider this much more carefully.

The second part is the people with whom the agent interacts.

The third part is the marketing environment. We interact with each other in a world filled with traffic, media messages, and bad weather. This stuff affects what we think and do, both by affecting our thoughts directly and by affecting us indirectly by affecting the people who affect us.

Taken together, the pieces of our story, or journey, make up the figure below:

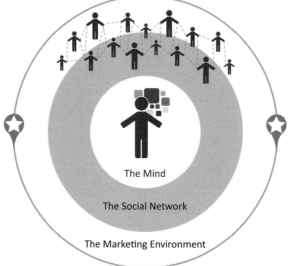

Figure 1: Concentric Circles in the Customer Journey

In the next three chapters that make up the first part of this book, we examine each of the three levels. Before we go on, however, we wish to emphasize one last point.

THE MOMENT OF DECISION IS ONLY ONE MOMENT

Marketers think that what they care about most is the moment of their consumer's purchasing decision. This is understandable, as this is when an individual decides to allocate his or her finite resources to your brand — or not.

But the decision to make a purchase depends only partly on the context at that particular moment. A lifetime of experiences has created the individual who, today, stands before a shelf of products, one of which is your brand. We rarely make choices following the classic rational choice model, in which we are assumed to carefully weigh all alternatives and their associated benefits and arrive at an "optimal decision." Instead, we are boundedly rational: we have preferences, but they can be swayed. We can be talked out of things. We have beliefs that sometimes make us very stubborn. We have emotions that can overtake us (and sometimes lead us to buy pre-packaged desserts). We behave following regular patterns — until we don't.

As we began this chapter, we need things and each day we satisfy them. Along the way we meet people, hear messages, try products, and form perceptions about them. Our reactions filter through our social network in bits and pieces of influence, which affect the behavior of others, which affects what we do, and what they do, and so on. Emotions and feelings are involved in two ways: they help define what we think our needs are (CHOCOLATE), and they help us determine among myriad choices what brands or products will satisfy us (Miracle Whip).

The moment of truth (the purchase) is a buildup of a lifetime of events, and from the moment after the purchase more experiences accumulate until the next one.

If you wish to sell a product to an individual, focusing just on the moment of truth is one option, but it means missing many others. It also poses an information problem: measuring brand perception and brand success based solely on the moment of purchase misses the point. How people think about, interact with, and behave based on the various brands and products in their lives is a much broader question than just: Did they buy it on that day at that place and hour?

From a brand perspective, any time an individual purchases your product, it's a moment where many interactive parts have come together to give rise to a single observable moment: a transaction. In between those moments, however, important actions, conversations, and changes take place. Studying the in-between is hard, but it's not impossible.

Your customers go on journeys every day, and today, you will come on one as well. By the end of this book, you will have been introduced to many different aspects of agent-based modeling (as well as physics, sociology, psychology, cognitive science, economics, and neuroscience), and you will be prepared to conduct your own agent-based modeling to better understand your customer, your competition, your brand, and the world they all exist in.

The Purchase Decision

OUR PLACE IN THE WORLD

To find out why people do what they do, we need to understand how they think. This is the innermost concentric circle. Later, we'll incorporate other influencers on behavior — such as friends and media messages — but these will all affect behavior through the filter of the mind.

While we can't know (yet) exactly how and when a particular person, message, or experience will trigger an emotional response, we can get quite close to approximating the process by which it happens. In this chapter we unpack that process through the components of the mind and the process with which those components are used in decision-making.

STEP 1: WHO CUSTOMERS ARE

All individuals in the world possess the following five things:

1. A background
2. A memory
3. A personality (no matter what you may have thought of your last blind date)
4. Opinions
5. Knowledge

We have each in different amounts and they take very different forms from person to person. But every single person has all five of these things, and all five play a role in how we react to information and other people, and how we translate those reactions to behaviors.

When we make choices about anything from what to eat for dinner to whether to go out for dinner, to whom we go with, to how we spend each and every single day — these choices are influenced to varying degrees by where we come from (background), what we remember (memory), what we know (knowledge), how we feel about things (opinion), and how those feelings are manifest (personality).

Again, this does not imply that we behave in ways that are predictable and rational. Rationality implies that we do things that are in our best interest, and theories of rationality are based on the assumption that when we make any decision, we calculate all possible outcomes, their associated probabilities, and the amount of benefit, or utility, we stand to gain from each option. Then we choose the best one.

The agent-based modeling view of individuals as rationally bounded is different. This view says that while we indeed go about the world seeking to make ourselves better off rather than worse off, we rarely know all possible outcomes, and we rarely conduct, or are even capable of conducting, all the calculations to choose the best ones. Instead, we make do with what we know. And what we know, again, comes from our background, memory, personality and opinions.

STEP 2: WHAT CUSTOMERS DO

An event is something that happens to us. It is triggered by something completely external — like an earthquake. Or it is caused by people in our social system — we hear a radio ad or have a nice dinner.

Individuals react to events that take place in the world. How we behave in our reactions comes from the five components above. Some events affect us because they remind us of something from our past, while they might slide right by another person unnoticed.

Some things make us angry while giving others comfort. It all comes back to our histories and our feelings.

When we follow behaviors that are reactions to events around us, we can do things that influence other people around us, like voice opinions loudly in a crowded market or persuade our friends to follow our lead. Or, we can do things that only indirectly affect others, like never buying a particular product again. This influences others only if our behavior aggregates with others to generate a change in sales, causing the brand to change how it interacts with current and potential customers.

A key point here is that our opinions, memory, personality, knowledge, and background do three things:

1. They differentiate us from other people.
2. They define how we react to stimuli.
3. They change in response to stimuli.

Building from the images in the previous chapter, we now have a world where diverse people interact and are affected by each other and by outside events.

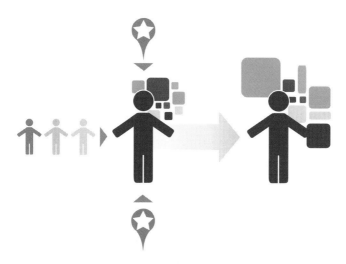

Figure 2: People and Events Influence Agent's Personalities, Opinions, Knowledge, and Memory

Now we can take those pieces and situate them in a context that more closely approximates the real world.

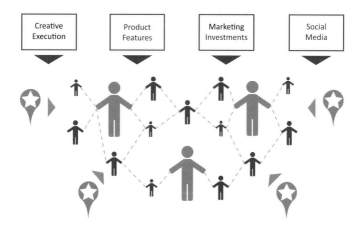

Figure 3: Agents Operate in Social Networks That Are Situated in Broader Contexts

HOW WE DECIDE

We have seen that individuals have memories and opinions that influence how they behave. There are three mechanisms through which memory and opinions can influence behavior. Here we consider the behavior of interest as the purchasing of a product. But the behavior can be anything — for whom you vote, where you go on vacation, or what you study in college (though all of these things can be thought of as purchasing behaviors).

The three mechanisms are: Preferences, Perceptions and Awareness.

Preferences are what we want. *Perceptions* are our ideas about whom or what will do it best. *Awareness* is whether we know about companies, people, or products that can satisfy what we want.

Preferences

Preferences are what we want in life — and what we want in a product. When individuals evaluate alternatives, they usually have a few attributes that are more important than others. Some people want really small computers, while others want really fast ones. Different personalities will give rise to different levels of importance associated with different attributes of products (say that ten times fast).

How we evaluate alternatives and which aspects we weigh more heavily than others will affect what we ultimately buy. And what you buy can affect what your friends buy, what individuals in your social network buy, and how the brand responds to purchasing behaviors. This can influence marketing campaigns, and can further impact what you buy. We're not quite saying you're the center of the universe, but we are saying that sometimes, under certain conditions, small actions (buying an electric toothbrush) can translate into macro effects (electronic toothbrushes become de rigueur and we all start to evaluate brushes according to new standards).

From a marketing perspective, the more you know about why any particular customer likes your product, the better off you'll be. From this view, it's not nearly enough to just know that someone purchased your product. Knowing what it was about the product that led them to their choice is where you really start to get some traction. Focus groups and surveys and proxy data can already help you get there, but combine that with nonlinear computational simulations and you're really onto something.

Perceptions

Preferences are how much you value product attributes. Perceptions are how you think a product measures up on different attributes. We all like to think that our perceptions are correct, but in reality we often carry biases based on a mix of personal history, personal information, and good old-fashioned stubbornness.

Even if our perceptions are not exactly accurate, they are the only ones we have, and thus guide our decisions. The existence of inaccurate perceptions and the reality that perceptions inform our behavior pose an important challenge for marketers.

The first challenge is that because of biases, asymmetric information, and unwillingness to learn at every step, new messages about your product may not necessarily cause a change in the beliefs of all message recipients. The second challenge is that if the messages are going to be received, they will only be successful in changing behavior if you've also gotten people's preferences right. A convincing message about improved product quality will resonate with people who care about quality, but not with those who care about fun.

Awareness

Having perceptions and preferences is all well and good, but if customers don't know your brand exists, you're not going to get terribly far. How do you invade the consciousness of a person? This is a big question. And if you do manage to do it — catch their attention for a blip in time on a billboard — how do you increase the probability that they remember your message?

The mechanisms, means, and processes by which humans accumulate, retain, and lose knowledge are the subject of much research in behavioral economics, neuroscience, psychology, and cognitive science. A lot of these have contributed to our understanding of how we learn, how we remember, and how we recall information.

Two major findings are that we all have finite attention and we are generally quick to forget. Just because someone is exposed to your message doesn't mean they'll remember it. It's also not necessarily the case that there is any kind of linear relationship between extent of exposure to a marketing message and probability of retaining it.

This isn't to say we always forget. We just usually do. This is not dismal news for you as a marketer, because customers are probably going to forget about your competitors, too. The more you are able to study how and when touchpoints from your campaign will influence customers, the more powerful your messages will be.

OUTCOMES

From a marketing perspective, we want to know what pieces of information go into the human brain, are made sense of in the mind, and then are translated into behaviors like making purchases. Combining our ever-growing knowledge of how the mind organizes and responds to reality with the principles of agent-based modeling — including networks, product reality, and competitive behavior — means we have never been better equipped to connect our innermost workings with our outermost actions.

As we will see in the chapter on agent-based modeling, we can build a probability engine that can translate the three big aspects of the mind into buying decisions, and measure not only purchasing outcomes, but further actions, like telling friends and strangers about our purchase.

Before we do that, we'd like to spend a bit more time elaborating on just how much goes into making a single choice.

AN APPLICATION: THE CAREFUL CRAFT OF PURCHASING A CAKE (AND YOU THOUGHT IT WAS EASY)

Sometimes we make purchases impulsively, unaware of the many factors influencing our decision. Other times we dwell endlessly in indecision, reading Internet reviews, calculating costs, harassing friends for advice, and weighing alternatives. No matter the process we experience when we make a choice, our knowledge, background, memory, opinions, and personality affect that choice. They do so by influencing our preferences over products, our perceptions of alternatives, and our awareness of what is out there for us.

Purchasing a single box of cake mix at the grocery store is very difficult. That is, it's difficult if we stick to a utility-maximizing rational choice model of decision-making, where individuals calculate the expected utility of all possible alternatives and select the one with the highest. This is easy for computers. It is difficult for humans. We will see that if, instead, we use a different model of decision making — one that uses bounded rationality — the decision can actually become easier, not harder. Limiting what we know and how much we consider in our choice sets help humans make most decisions with far less cognitive effort than true calculations require. Is ignorance bliss? Maybe.

At any major grocery store there is a full wall of cake mix boxes. For tractability, we will not even consider the frosting, candles, and ice cream that will eventually be needed to accompany it. You'll thank us for this. After the calculation is complete, however, we will insist you purchase a pint of ice cream and consume it while crying softly in your kitchen in a mix of relief and exhaustion.

Where were we? Ah, yes. We were about to back up a touch. On top of your choice of cake mix, your decision to go to this grocery store in the first place means you somehow settled on this one instead of the other 25+ in your town. Your choice was made based on some mix of preference for proximity to your home, price of products on the shelves, the quality of those products, location of the store, and your store experience. This alone is a dazzling array of factors influencing a simple decision. It's a decision most of us make without even thinking about for more than a moment every now and again.

Meanwhile, suppose we've made it to the grocery store, having not only chosen which destination, but also the route to get there (which also comes from a variety of factors and results in exposure to very different scenes, people, and marketing messages).

Now you must choose between cakes. The simpler choice is one available in the grocery store. But what if, while you're there, you (dangerously) allow your mind to wander to other options, not necessarily confined to your store? At your own risk, consider the following.

The top ten results pages on an amazon.com search for cake mix yields 60 brands (see List 1 for a fascinating journey through the names of all of these). The average grocery store in the United States (based on a search of Safeway, the third largest grocery store chain in the U.S.) carries approximately 10 brands of dry cake mixes, plus a variety of pre-made cakes, frozen cakes, in-house customizable cakes from the bakery, or even additional ones you might be able to order.

Among the cake mix brands, some of the top ones make as many as 25 different types of cakes. Duncan Hines makes 25 different kinds of cakes. Betty Crocker makes 23. (See List 2 and 3 for details on the products of these two companies.) Other companies (mercifully) don't make nearly as many: Arrowhead Mills, for example, makes only three different flavors (how quaint).

We haven't even gotten into the different types of places that sell cakes: bakeries are an obvious choice, but coffee shops and tea houses can carry them, as can restaurants, catering services, and ice cream parlors. Gas stations and convenience stores can also carry them (this is not to say we necessarily endorse you sending your loved ones TastyCakes for their birthdays).

Your final decision, the cake mix you purchase from a particular retailer, is one among (very approximately) more than 25 (stores in a town) x 10 (brands in a store) x 3 (average number of flavors per brand) x 20 (other in-store cake alternatives) x 65 (brands on the Internet) x 3 (average flavors of brands on the Internet) x 10 (other non-grocery cake selling spots) x 5 (average number of cake choices at all those other spots) =

146,250,000 possible cake and cake purchasing location choices!

Of course, the numbers here will vary from place to place and are rough estimations. But the idea holds. Even if you reduce these numbers considerably, it's still a lot of alternatives.

Of course, we don't consider all of these when we make a decision. Many we can rule out instantly: I don't want a gluten free, low fat, vanilla, store-bought, or expensive cake mix. And I always go to Safeway no matter what. And I'm probably not going to consider a gas station.

Instantly, the decision is winnowed down tremendously, to the point where it's (almost) plausible to calculate the rest in store on your phone's calculator.

The process by which you narrowed down those choices, however, is incredibly important. From a marketing perspective, that's where the difference between success and loss lies. If you are a marketer for Wal-Mart and can understand why a person would always go to Safeway no matter what, and alter that — well, you just got yourself a new customer. Do that a whole bunch and we'll see people trekking across the city to get to Wal-Mart.

We're going to use this moment to make an interesting point. We are going to suggest to you that there is no such thing as true brand loyalty.

Backing off a bit: to be more specific, we'll allow that there is actually no such thing as brand loyalty in a permanent sense. (What is loyalty if not permanent, you ask? We're not sure, either. Ask a divorce lawyer.)

Brand "loyalty" can exist in an ephemeral and mostly illusionary fashion for a time. People can look awfully loyal to Duncan Hines for a long time, but if Betty Crocker comes up with something better and cheaper, most of that "loyalty" will go to Ms. Crocker. What we call brand loyalty may be better captured as "temporary or medium-run brand enthusiasm." (Do you take Betty Crocker to be your temporary or medium-run object of general enthusiasm? You may now kiss the box.)

Luckily for us, humans are not wired to calculate things like computers do. We see, sense, feel, and believe. We cry during moving television advertisements and laugh at funny Internet videos about products as simple as towels and cornstarch. Sometimes we're attracted to the color red, other times we only buy what we bought last time. We're messy creatures when it comes to making decisions, and scientists have spent decades crafting a deep understanding of the way we make choices despite (or in fact, because of) this beautiful mess. Calling this decision process bounded rationality makes the marketing problem a lot friendlier, as it acknowledges our "rational" limits and allows us to account for them. (Interestingly, bounded rationality is really hard for computers. See Andy Clark's book in the Read Further section at the end of this chapter.)

THE IMPORTANCE OF CATEGORIES

It's easy to state that how we think affects how we behave. But how do we think? One major way is by making categories, into which we sort different things we see in the world. When evaluating brands and products, a first step that comes prior to all of the above considerations, like perception and awareness, is putting products into categories to be evaluated. We'll come back to this point in later chapters on product development and marketing strategies.

Market categories are necessary, but they are actually illusions — and being able to change the category in which your product is considered is itself a tool of marketing. Until those later discussions, we introduce the subject here in this discussion of the mind. Because we love it, we're going to keep using cakes as our example du jour.

According to a mix of Wikipedia and popular lore, there are six major cake shapes: layer cakes, sheet cakes, cupcakes, bundt cakes, swiss roll cakes, and cake balls. All the classics.

We can also classify cakes in endlessly different ways. If we classify them by primary ingredient, we have yeast cakes (such as babka or stollen), cheesecakes, sponge cakes, butter cakes, or fruit cakes. There is also a vicious debate in the caking community about whether it is legitimate to classify them by their accompaniment; e.g., a coffee cake. (Please pass the vodka cake?)

We could even classify cakes by ingredients they do not contain; e.g., a flourless cake or a gluten-free cake. Be warned: the legitimacy of this practice is also a hotly debated matter. We advise that you not bring it up unless in close company. Even then you may be surprised to learn of your loved one's views.

We can also classify them by purpose: birthday cakes, wedding cakes, graduation cakes. There's also Passover plava, mooncakes, and, according to Duncan Hines anyway, Halloween cakes. We don't know about funeral cakes, layoff cakes, or estranged lover cakes, but feel free to consider them.

This exercise may seem silly, but it speaks to some broad observations a lot of smart and serious thinkers have made about the world around us and how humans think about and make sense of that world. What is a cake? How do we determine what is and is not a cake? (This is a more important question than you may have been led to understand.)

Once we've decided our categories, how do humans choose between them? How can marketing messages facilitate that choice? How can marketing change the very factors that go into human calculations as they make that choice?

We know that a wedding cake and a stollen loaf have more in common with each other than with a tennis ball. But they certainly are not the same thing, and with the exception, we are sure, of some places in both rural Germany and rural Pennsylvania, they are not interchangeable. But, if someone who makes stollen could convince the average American that stollen is an ideal choice for a wedding cake (hey, they are good), they could make a great deal of money.

Before we go on, we also want to point out that we haven't even brought up pies, beefcakes, pudding, brownies, cookies, or cakewalks. You're welcome. Is a cake more like a pie or a cookie? Families have been torn apart over this.

The important thing is: a major way humans make sense of the world is by making categories, and once these categories are made, we tend to evaluate things within categories far more often than between them. But this doesn't mean they are permanent.

THE MIND, MARKETING, AND COMPLEXITY

Agent-based modeling allows for consideration of events that have very low probabilities. Even if unlikely, every brand and every style of cake that exists on Earth has some probability of being selected (even the one you buried in the backyard as a child, and even the one the U.S. government sent to space in a time capsule).

Marketing is a means of changing the minds of people so that the probability that they purchase your product increases. If a marketer for a particular cake that is hidden in the deepest corner of the grocery store, the Internet, or the universe does it right, he/she can make customers respond. There are almost no zero probabilities — only low probabilities waiting to grow.

A traditional way of thinking typically holds that the marketer is in control of things and there is order to the world. Pull one lever and see the expected outcome. We increasingly are realizing that this view of the world is not quite right. There is certainly some order in the world (we'll learn more about this in Chapter 3), but it's not how we thought it looked. There are patterns that lie somewhere between randomness and perfect predictability. The trick is less about pinpointing particular outcomes with some probability and more about understanding the processes and conditions that give rise to particular patterns.

The idea that we can be in complete control — or hold things constant and see the effects we want actually borne out — is no longer the only view available to us. The dynamic, patterned, evolving world in which we live is influenced by us and we are influenced by it, but we cannot be the conductor of the show. We also need to not just go along for the ride. If we understand what's coming and why, we can make it work for us.

IN SUMMARY: ALGORITHMS OF THE MIND

You might buy with some probability any brand that is in your choice set. There is a distribution. Until now we were relegated to assuming the distribution was reliable.

It actually is not. The workings of the human mind and what areas of the brain contribute to decision-making and our resulting behaviors, is an ongoing area of study by neurologists and neuroscientists; researchers have uncovered the specific areas of the somatosensory cortex that are responsible for decision-making and control over behavior.

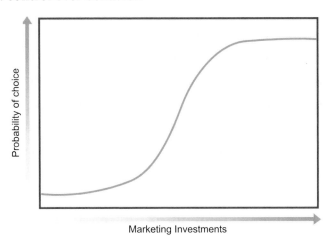

Figure 4:
The Swing Vote Nature of How Customers Behave

Some people in a market can be swayed to purchase your product. Some always will, and some never will, but they don't matter to you (at least not nearly as much, see figure 4). In the chapter on the social network, we will outline how the marketer does not have full control over who is swayed or not. Other people can also affect your customers. Friends, neighbors and fellow citizens of the world have influence as well.

The mind is a partial information system. It can only prioritize so much. The mind doesn't resolve preference once — it is forever running parallel processing of all the information it receives. It is the individual making decisions on partial information in rational and irrational ways that sets everything in motion.

Read Further

Clark, Andy. 1998. *Being There: Putting Brain, Body, and the World Together Again.* Cambridge: The MIT Press.

Damasio, Antonio R. 1995. *Descartes' Error: Emotion, Reason, and the Human Brain.* New York: Harper Perennial.

Kahneman, Daniel, Paul Slovic, and Amos Tversky. 1982. *Judgment Under Uncertainty: Heuristics and Biases.* Cambridge: Cambridge University Press.

LIST 1:
FOR YOUR ENJOYMENT, 60 BESTSELLING CAKE BRANDS ON AMAZON.COM
(from top 250 search results for "cake mix" of 877 total results, as of January 2011)

1. Betty Crocker	22. Sweet 'n Low
2. Libby's	23. Quick-Bake
3. Pamela's Products	24. NordicWare
4. Fisher	25. Dean Jacobs
5. Xcell	26. Mary Lake-Thompson Ltd.
6. Namaste Foods	27. Stonewall Kitchen
7. Zebra Mix	28. Aunt Jemima
8. Bob's Red Mill	29. Krusteaz
9. Canterbury Naturals	30. Fast & Fresh
10. FiberGourmet	31. Kinnikinnick
11. Cherrybrook Kitchen	32. Naturally Nora
12. The Cravings Place	33. 123 Gluten Free
13. Barefoot Contessa	34. Bernard
14. Carnival	35. The King's Cupboard
15. Duncan Hines	36. Pillsbury
16. Gluten-Free Pantry	37. Beallsflorida
17. Arrowhead Mills	38. Garvey's
18. Dassant	39. Dixie Carb Counters
19. Jell-o	40. Gluuteny
20. Simply Organic	41. Sweets4U2
21. Oetker	42. The Invisible Chef

43. Dean Jacobs

44. Dowd & Rogers

45. Ya-Hoo Baking Company

46. Jiffy

47. Canterbury Naturals

48. Sof'ella Gourmet Natural

49. OrgaN

50. Hodgson Mill

51. The Prepared Pantry

52. Authentic Foods Baking Mix

53. Patisse

54. The Heartland, Inc

55. WOW Baking Company

56. Caledonian Kitchen

57. San Sucre

58. Jotis62.Cause You're Special

59. Paula Deen Collection

60. Well and Good

LIST 2:
SAMPLE OF CAKE FLAVORS OF A TOP BRAND —
DUNCAN HINES

1. Apple Caramel
2. Classic Carrot
3. Triple Chocolate
4. Angel Food
5. Moist Deluxe Butter Recipe Golden
6. Classic White
7. Classic Yellow
8. French Vanilla
9. Caramel
10. Confetti Cupcake
11. Spice Premium
12. Tres Leche
13. Fudge
14. Dark Chocolate Fudge
15. Devil's Food
16. Fudge Marble
17. German Chocolate
18. Red Velvet
19. Swiss Chocolate
20. Banana Supreme
21. Coconut Supreme
22. Lemon Supreme
23. Orange Supreme
24. Pineapple Supreme
25. Strawberry Supreme

There are also 482 recipes at duncanhines.com for what to do with these flavors.

LIST 3:
CATEGORIES OF CAKES ACCORDING TO BETTY CROCKER

1. Birthday cakes
2. Birthday cupcakes
3. Brunch cakes
4. Bundt cakes
5. Cakes with fruit
6. Cheesecakes
7. Chocolate cakes
8. Christmas cakes
9. Cupcakes
10. Frosted cakes
11. Frosted cupcakes
12. Frozen cakes
13. Gold Medal flour cakes
14. Halloween cakes
15. Halloween cupcakes
16. Ice cream cakes
17. Kids' cakes
18. Kids' cupcakes
19. Springform pan cakes
20. Springform pan cheesecakes
21. SuperMoist angel food cakes
22. Bundt pan SuperMoist recipes
23. SuperMoist cake mixes
24. SuperMoist cupcakes
25. SuperMoist poke cakes

The Social Network

WE ARE ALL CONNECTED

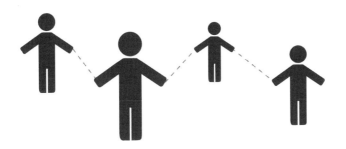

We've just seen how many factors inside one person's mind interact to give rise to different behaviors. Other people also affect our behavior.

People you know, people you don't know, and people very far away also affect what you do in every single moment, including making purchasing decisions. Others can affect you directly by giving you advice. Thousands of people affect your decisions every time you read a product review on the Internet. The clothes you observe strangers wear, the things people say on television, and the stories that make the news headlines each morning all contribute to what and how we think about the world.

Due in part to their power in changing marketing results, you have probably already heard of networks. Many popular books about the science and importance of networks are readily available in bookstores across the country (see the end of this chapter for a short list). In this chapter, we cover just a few of the most important aspects of networks that can help you see just how powerful they are — and how, because of advances in science and technology — you can use them to your competitive advantage.

Many people are using the science of networks to solve some of our world's most pressing social problems: from the AIDS epidemic to charity donations to earthquake victims to religiosity and political preferences — better understanding of the networks that affect these outcomes means better solutions.

WHOM DO YOU KNOW?

The simple and accidental act of running into a friend on the street can change how you spend your day. Your friend may mention a new restaurant, a new product from a grocery store, or casually reference an upcoming vacation. This is a completely unplanned and unexpected occurrence, but if it influences your decision to check out a new restaurant, buy a new product, or contemplate how to save for a vacation, it has profound consequences for what you do, where you go, and where you spend your money.

If the character from the story in the introductory chapter had not heard from someone else who had a positive experience with baking a cake that day, the person would have gone to a bakery and had a stranger put together a concoction of sweets. Instead, a cake mix company and a humble grocery store received the business. If after the cake was served, the character started a conversation on the Internet with some friends or posted a product review, it's likely even more people would be influenced to make a purchase they would not have otherwise.

As we saw in the last chapter, for marketers it is extremely important to know not just when a product generates conversation, but also when those conversations translate into purchases. This chapter focuses on the first task: how conversations are started in the first place. If you want to influence someone, you tell him or her something. How do messages spread around the world? What can we understand about the spread of information? How can we use this knowledge to our advantage? What is still left to learn?

MARKETING AND THE SCIENCE OF NETWORKS

You probably already know that social networks are powerful. You know that things like buzz, viral videos, conversations between friends, social influence, brand loyalists and brand entrepreneurs, and dozens of other actors, people, and concepts all either matter or seem like they matter in predicting consumer behavior.

You also know that there are many ways you can reach out to your customers and potential customers: TV, radio, newsprint, social networking sites, Internet ads, email messages, text messages, billboards, t-shirts, coffee cup sleeves, car flyers, event sponsorship, and much more. The number of ways you can connect with customers is limited only by your own imagination.

The question is: Which media tools are best suited for which marketing goals for customers in what kinds of networks? Just because Facebook exists does not mean it will be an effective marketing platform for your brand. And just because coffee sleeves with ads are clever, this also does not mean they will help you. To know what will help, you need to know three things:

1. The structure of how your customers are connected to one another and to information outlets

2. The extent to which different touchpoints reach different segments of your target population

3. The number of other messages against which you will compete for customers' attention. (We'll address this third part in Chapter 7 where we consider the role of competition)

Until now, we've had to rely solely on the past to answer these questions. Marketers are understandably terrified about making a wrong move. To learn about what works we've had to roll out media campaigns and measure changes in purchases. We couldn't attribute results to the inner workings of what took place between the moment of airing an ad and a consumer's decision at the supermarket.

Even more frighteningly, we had to assume that if sales went up, our ad was good. How could we not? Because of this, we get tied to particular campaigns and metrics and use them again and again. We grow afraid to innovate until we're forced to. We drove forward looking through the rearview mirror.

A RELUCTANT INNOVATOR NO MORE

The new science of networks and corresponding computational tools to understand networks mean you are about to be a lot more powerful and a lot bolder than before. There are currently real, concrete ways we can measure and evaluate the networks in which our customers live, how the networks affect the messages they see, and how the messages they see affect future behavior, like spreading the word about a product.

Below are a few of the top concepts. As you will see, they are intuitive and measurable, and help lend insight to the processes that give rise to word-of-mouth, trends, viral videos — and the opposite: lack of attention, indifference, and silence. The more we know about networks — including how their structure affects the spread of information across it, how information affects their structure, and how all of it affects an individual mind — the more we can understand when to expect fads, when to expect permanent popularity, and when to expect flops.

CONCEPTS IN THE SCIENCE OF NETWORKS

Advances in the science of networks have produced a great deal of work that covers many aspects of networks. Many books have been written to introduce interested readers to major concepts in networks, so we won't spend a great deal of time here discussing them. Instead, we introduce the major concepts.

Building Blocks: Edges and Nodes

The people, places, or things that make up a network are called nodes in the science of networks, and we represent connections between them in graphics using lines called edges. A network is a representation of the interconnection of elements. Social networks include people, but even they can also include companies, governments, or brands. Anything we interact with in any regularity could belong in a social network. These interactions can be in-person meetings, phone calls, emails, tweets, or seeing someone on television.

We can also draw networks of almost anything — from whales to chimps to doctors. We can draw the network of connections between neurons in the brain. We can draw connections between computers linked over the Internet or a company network.

Networks can also be directed or undirected. Directed networks are ones where information, influence, or energy flows from one actor to another. Information from the news flows to listeners over a directed network. Undirected networks are ones where information flows back and forth. Chats with your coworkers over lunch would be represented by information flowing in an undirected network.

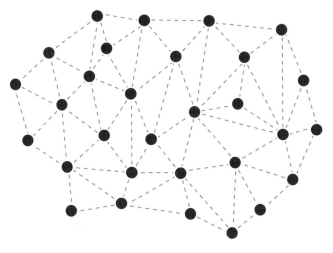

Figure 5:
An Undirected Social Network

Even this simple mapping of the components of a network and how they fit together illustrates that a good understanding of networks can contribute to a much richer understanding of how information might flow to people, and how it might flow between them. When we get into more advanced chapters, we'll consider how a good feedback structure in the network between you and your customers can help you tailor your messages and your product to your customers more quickly than your competition. A really advanced chapter (the next book?) might consider how marketers could tailor their messages so that the very network changes as a result of information flow.

Density

With how many people do you interact on any given day? How many people do you hear from in some way — via the Internet, your phone, and through email? How many people do you hear from whom you don't know — in magazine advertisements, on TV, on billboards, on the radio? Density is a measure of how many social contacts you have, and we can tune it to include just close friends, or everyone who might connect with you on some level. Density is a ratio: it's the number of people in a network to whom you're connected, divided by the total number of people. The more connections you have relative to total population, the more dense the network.

What does this mean for marketing? Information tends to spread more quickly over dense networks. As we'll continue to impress upon you, marketing is about information speed, feedback, and an ability to both look ahead and adapt to changes. In fact, that's what most of life is about (well, that and picnics, and champagne).

Compare the below two images to see how density matters.

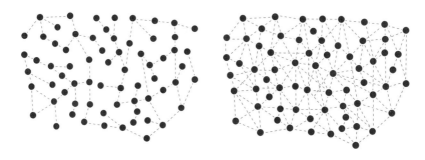

Figure 6:
Less Dense vs. More Dense Network

Even though messages can generally spread more quickly in a dense social network, we must also consider the fact that messages can be good or bad. Therefore, it is important to further clarify the importance and relevance of social density from a marketing perspective. If you roll out a product that ends up underwhelming most of your customers, you would prefer that they are in less dense social networks.

Randomness

Connections between people are neither perfectly random nor perfectly ordered. They are somewhere in the middle. You don't find friends completely at random, but you also don't acquire friends in a perfectly predictable pattern. While there is usually some pattern to how we found most of our friends, we can't perfectly predict the development of these relationships, nor can we insist that all friendships are created along the same pattern. With whom we are friends is *kind of* predictable. That is, it produces patterns that we can describe, measure, and anticipate with some probability, though usually without exact point estimation.

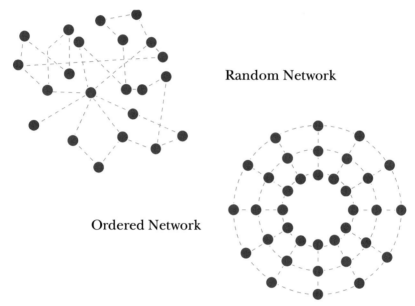

Random Network

Ordered Network

Figure 7: Random and Ordered Networks

In addition to measuring the connections between customers, we can go further by describing patterns within these social networks. One of the most common patterns created by people in social groups is called small world networks. Small world networks refer to networks where most people have a slightly below average number of connections, and just a few people have a very high number.

Consider the illustration of a small world network below:

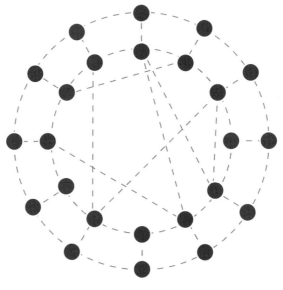

Figure 8:
Small World Network

It is easy to see why a message might spread more quickly across a small world network than across either the random or ordered networks from above. As shown in Figure 9, if you begin at position A, the average number of steps that must be taken in order to reach anyone else in the network is two. We can see that in this case, the number of steps from A to B is five. In a random network, the average is higher. In an ordered one, it is also higher.

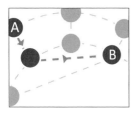
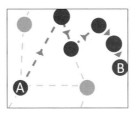
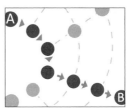

Path from A to B in
a Small World Network

Path from A to B in
a Random Network

Path from A to B in
an Ordered Network

Figure 9:
Network Paths

The reason small world networks are relevant to marketers is that information spreads more quickly across a small world network than it does over many other types of social networks. For example, if everyone is clustered without faraway ties, messages introduced to that group will just ricochet around those same people over and over again.

There's one more concept we'll add in here: Strong and weak ties, or links, in a network. A weak link is someone to whom you're connected, but not directly. It's someone who is a friend of a friend. A strong link is your friend. Interestingly, it turns out, weak links matter a lot when it comes to spreading messages through populations. If people were only influenced by those with whom they had strong links, we'd never learn anything new. We need weak ties. And marketers, keep this in mind as we move to the next section on influence in networks. Weak ties are your friends — figuratively.

Will your message just rocket around the same nine people, or will it get conveyed over weak ties? Or will weak ties be created because of your message? Media messages can build connections between people.

In sum, if you know the kind of network in which your customers live and connect, you can target your media marketing mix, your non-media campaigns, and the very features of the product itself such that it exploits this network and runs like wildfire on its own network propelled energy. Get the network wrong, and you may find your product never becomes more popular than it currently is. Or as we'll see in future chapters, your product is forgotten. Will you disappear? Or will you remain a vibrant part of the network — even, as hinted above, helping forge new connections?

Many Networks

What a network looks like affects how powerful your message can be. It's also possible for your message to affect what the network looks like.

If you already have some familiarity with networks in your business, you may be tempted to think you already know this stuff. Networks have been really popular for some time, indeed, but in our experience most companies are misusing networks. They are hinking: my customers are connected and therefore they will talk.

Not so. How are they connected? When do they talk? Why do they talk? You need to know this to make networks useful for you.

Your customers live in different networks for different products.

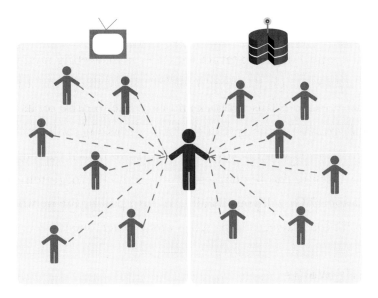

Figure 10:
Network for Talking about TV Shows — Network for Talking about Cake

There certainly may be much overlap in the two networks above, but they are not the same. Knowing just that already gets you ahead of the competition. The different networks in which we live and learn matter in terms of predicting how information will flow across them.

Probability of Interaction

The final network concept concerns the probability of interaction. If you have ten favorite friends, they might appear on a mapping of your social network as one node away from you. But, chances are, you do not interact with them all equally. Maybe some live in the same city as you, while others do not.

And even among those who live near you, there may be some who are closer in age to you, or who share more interests with you, or whose opinions about various things you regard more highly.

These few would be more influential on you than the others for two reasons. The first is that you're simply more likely to interact. This comes from the network structure that we've just described. The second is that some people are simply more influential than others, and this is a fact independent from network structure.

It may be the case that, regardless of the status of your shared or divergent issues, one of your sisters is just more likely to speak her mind, share her opinion, or offer you advice. She's the one who calls you up to recommend a new restaurant after she tried it the night before, or the one who volunteers information about a great sale going on at a luxury department store. She's more charismatic and, thus, by almost none of your own doing, you are more influenced by her.

Complexity and network science also address these features of networks — the fact that not all nodes are equal. Next, we consider a few of the most important reasons why it matters who is at the other end of our edge.

HUMAN NETWORKS ARE HUMAN

Not all connections are created equal. Even weak ties and strong ties don't get us nearly far enough in understanding the rich and diverse ways we connect with others.

Thousands of voices are around us all the time. But we can only listen to so many people at a time. What messages from what people get through to us?

A great deal of research suggests that we usually give more priority to the people closest to us — physically and emotionally — but every so often something random will move us. Strangers can be oddly powerful people.

■ How do we know who is going to influence us today?

From a marketing perspective, how can you make sure you are the one doing the most influencing? Here are a few concepts from research in interpersonal influence (which spans psychology, sociology, political science, and economics) that are useful in thinking about who is sending messages and how they influence others.

Charisma

You don't take advice from just anybody. Just because you run into a friend on the street doesn't mean you're going to do what he says. It matters to whom you talk, and whom you ignore. Furthermore, you ask different people for advice about different things.

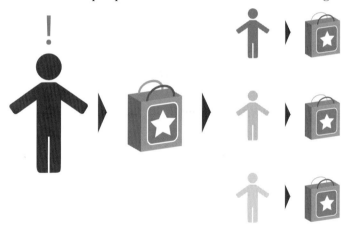

Figure 11:
Charisma and Consumer Preference

Someone who is charismatic is someone to whom you're more likely to listen. Charismatic people have a personality that you admire, respect, or want to emulate for any number of deep, dark, mysterious, or shallow reasons. They can be strangers or close friends. They can even be you.

Influentials

If you talk to someone who tends to have good taste, or whose opinion you respect, or is someone like you, or is someone with whom you enjoy talking, or who is especially persuasive — you are more likely to be influenced by him or her. The influentials hypothesis holds that some people are more trusted about a particular issue and, thus, opinions tend to change to match these people in a network.

Figure 12:
Marketers and Influentials

Therefore, if you want to increase the spread of awareness of a product or change opinions about a product, you would do well to contact the most influential people first. This also means that the well-connected people who are most influential would be the most attractive market segment to target, given their influence over others in the social network.

Who are the influentials? Experts? People with strong rhetorical skills? People who have attractive personalities? People who are just plain attractive? And what determines who is influential to whom? Again, who is influential depends on the topic under discussion. We turn to the idea of the diffusion of innovations to unpack this a bit more.

Diffusion of Innovation

Media Campaign

Friends

Figure 13:
Social and Paid Media Influence on Consumers

Sometimes we make decisions based on the advice of our friends. Other times we reach conclusions on our own. Sometimes we are the most influential people we know. Indeed, we carry around all of our biases, preferences, and stubborn ways with us everywhere we go. Sometimes external influences don't carry as much weight as our internal biases and preferences.

Customers can hear about a new product through traditional media campaigns on television, radio, or the Internet, and then decide to purchase the product or service independently of any word-of-mouth mechanism.

Marketing is one part of a conversation that people have with each other. It can become a means to connect. Or it can distract and irritate.

CONSUMER POWER

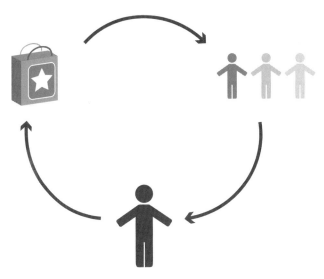

Figure 14:
Brand and Consumer Power

People aren't simply information sponges. Individuals also gather and share information with one another. You can talk to friends about a product experience, or you might post about it online. You can also be proactive in seeking information — for example, you might read reviews or information about a product on the Internet. The new view of marketing assigns power to customers. Customers are no longer passive recipients only. They are part of the conversation.

A true social network includes both the propensity of others to influence you and your propensity to influence others. And as we see in **Figure 14** on page 57, the extent to which you both affect and are affected depends on your personality, the personality of others, differences in opinions, and the structure of the network over which you interact in the first place.

CONCLUSION: WHO AFFECTS YOU?

An inquiry into a social network is at its deepest level a question of who affects whom. We are regularly touched, affected, changed, inspired, and influenced by others. What causes someone to have an effect on you has until now seemed the domain of magic and speculation.

The convergence of advances in agent-based modeling and insight from rigorous work in networks theory have allowed us to directly analyze how information and ideas flow between people. As we have seen, they flow according to three major principles. Note that the third one in particular builds from work in the mind from the previous chapter.

1. The structure of the network. How are we connected?

2. The level of charisma and influence of actors in the structure of the network. How are we connected?

3. Individual levels of receptivity to influence. How strong are our own beliefs and preferences? (Are we sources or sinks of information?) What kind of people are we?

This chapter has covered the first and second questions. In the previous chapter we delved headfirst (get it?!) into the human mind. Decisions are the target of influence for all true marketers, from political candidates to college recruiters to a door-to-door vacuum cleaner salesman. We all want to influence beliefs, yes, but we really only care about them when they translate into decisions that influence behavior.

For now, let's recap. We've covered a lot of different terms and introduced you to pieces of the science of networks. What do you do with these ideas and principles? How do you connect all these pieces?

What You Can Do

If you can give a reasonable estimate as to the randomness of the network and the edge distribution, this will determine the average degree of separation and the number of hubs.

The segments of the population and their relative proportions, initial opinions, and experience with the product will determine the direction of influence and who holds it. The product category itself tells you how much people talk about it.

Put it together and you can discover how quickly word of mouth spreads, what its impact is, and who is responsible for it. What you find may surprise you. You may find that influentials or people at hubs are important, but that they are meaningless without approval from an expert at the periphery. Or you might find that hubs are meaningless and your information will trickle through the population no matter what the structure.

Information of any kind in this regard will help you tailor and target your marketing campaign.

A FINAL WORD ON NETWORKS

It is a truism in much of poetry and literature that it is the people who make up our lives who affect us most. This is true to an extent. Our conversations with one another ebb and flow in mentions of products without us even realizing it. When we are inspired by someone to bake a cake, this is primarily an emotional experience, drawing from feelings as mixed as mutual respect, personal memories, and excitement about the unknown. The decision to purchase cake mix is a byproduct of a host of experiences.

This is nothing short of a science of how we are moved by others. That it helps us to better sell our products is a beneficial side effect. With complexity, we begin to be able to plan profundity.

There is a philosophy around social networks, and the framework introduced here connects disparate parts in a way that has never before been done. Many have studied each or several of these concepts very deeply. We have brought them together so we can learn from them. The more we understand about how network structure, the people in the network, and the human mind all influence each other, the more power we have to use them all for good.

Read Further

Barabasi, Albert-Laszlo. 2003. *Linked: How Everything Is Connected to Everything Else and What It Means.* New York: Plume.

Newman, M. E. J. 2010. *Networks: An Introduction.* Oxford: Oxford University Press.

Newman, M. E. J., Albert-Laszlo Barabasi, and Duncan J. Watts. 2006. *The Structure and Dynamics of Networks* (Princeton Studies in Complexity). Princeton: Princeton University Press.

Newman, M. E. J. 2005. *"Power Laws, Pareto Distributions, and Zipf's Law."* Contemporary Physics 46, 323-351

Watts, Duncan J. 2003. *Six Degrees: The Science of a Connected Age.* New York: W. Norton & Company, Inc.

CHAPTER FOUR

Concepts in Complexity

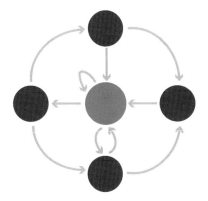

S o far we have established that humans are driven by their minds, which hold their background, knowledge, opinions, personality, and memory. And we know that perceptions, preferences, and awareness influence how the contents of the mind translate into behavior.

We also know that humans do not exist in a vacuum, or out floating in space. Each of us is a part of a social network, and many sub-networks. These networks contain everything from our friends and family to our colleagues and neighbors, to friends of friends, and even to companies whose messages affect us through touchpoints. The structure of our network, including how many connections we have and what kind, affects how information flows through our network.

Our network also does not exist in the ether. It is embedded in a changing environment that is characterized by unexpected events, constraints on resources, and both a waxing and a waning of things like wealth, fashion trends, and optimism. We live in a dynamic environment that both affects us and is affected by us.

More specifically, we affect the environment when our behaviors and interactions lead to macro level outcomes characterized by changes in the environment. The environment affects us when new circumstances give us new information about how to behave. Humans adapt to environmental changes. When prices go up, we buy less. When the weather gets better, we go outside more.

How the behaviors of individuals affect aggregate outcomes and how those outcomes in turn affect individuals is the stuff of agent-based modeling. Agent-based modeling is a technique to aid the study of complex systems. A complex system is a collection of diverse, interacting, adaptive parts whose interactions give rise to unpredictable and often surprising, but patterned, big events. The interactions between parts of the system affect the total system, which then affect the parts.

There are many interesting and important properties of complex systems, but the ones we will focus on most are the unexpected events and patterns that complex systems produce. This has implications for how we make predictions. Making predictions in complex systems tends to involve looking for patterns and understanding the circumstances that give rise to them. Point predictions with associated confidence intervals, which we use in traditional statistics, carry less meaning when we are dealing with complex systems.

In this chapter we introduce four concepts that are regularly used to describe outcomes and properties of complex systems. These are not all there are, but mastering these four will give anyone a working knowledge of the major ideas behind complex systems, what they are, and what we can gain by studying them.

EMERGENCE

Emergence is as close to the idea of getting something from nothing as we can get. It's something big coming from really small pieces.

Emergence is the idea that the whole is greater than the sum of its parts. A less common, but still apt, way to think of emergence is sort of like a magic trick: introduce several variables into a hat, let them mix around, and voila, out comes a rabbit — or, in this case, a pattern of improved perceptions about your brand.

If this has so far sounded vague, it's for good reason: many complexity scientists have spent a great deal of effort trying to define emergence, and there exist almost as many definitions of emergence as there are complexity scientists, if not more. One of the first books about emergence, *Emergence*, by John Holland, is spectacularly insightful and prompted decades of work on the concept. Even it does not contain a definition of emergence.

(Check out the recommended reading at the end of this chapter and find out for yourself. That said, if you finish reading the book, you have experienced what emergence is. The definition of emergence, thus, is itself an emergent property of the combination of about 20,000 words and graphics.)

But, we don't want to leave you hanging. Here's a working definition. Emergence refers to the process by which the interaction of different elements gives rise to (causes) the creation of something new — usually an unexpected and unpredictable, completely different entity from any of its composite parts.

■ **Try saying that three times fast — again!**

Emergence also almost always results from processes that are nonlinear. Before we break down the definition even more, here are a few examples of things that are emergent:

A Flock of Birds: This is the result of independent movement of many birds, yet the result acts as a whole.

Consciousness: This arises from the interactions of the firing of many neurons and brain tissue. The result is the ability to think.

Disease Epidemics: The interactions of many people, some of whom are infected, give rise to the broad and measurable phenomenon that is an epidemic.

Brand Equity: Surely you saw this one coming. The popularity and salience of a brand comes about from the interaction of media messages, individual purchasing decisions, communications between people, and features of the brand itself.

■ Here are a few things that are not emergent.

A Cake: We know. We wish they were emergent, too. Instead, they are perfectly predictable based on the combination of ingredients used. Yes, they all turn out a little bit different from one another, and things like altitude, pan type, ingredient quality, and oven temperatures can affect that. But overall, what you put in more or less results in what you get. A chemical reaction is not the same thing as emergence. At the same time, taste is emergent. The interactions of the components of a recipe lead to a completely different taste not found in any ingredient alone.

A Car: There are many working parts in a car, all of which add up exactly to a car. Traffic, on the other hand, is an emergent outcome of the interaction of many individual cars (and drivers)!

A House: A collection of concrete, shingles, and furniture results in something that is very complicated (and costly to maintain), but not complex. What you put into a house is what you get out. A "home," on the other hand, is arguably an emergent outcome of a house plus the interaction of people and beliefs. Things like segregation and housing market prices are also emergent phenomena that arise from collections of houses and the people in them.

Love: Just kidding. We don't know anything about love, either. Maybe it is emergent.

A rule of thumb is: Things that result in a linear, predictable, or otherwise "normal" fashion are not emergent. Things that come about in unexpected swells, or that take on unexpected characteristics that bear almost nothing to the interacting parts, are emergent.

You can also think about emergence sometimes as a kind of robustness. This isn't the same thing as emergence, but it is related. If a few tweaks to one or more variables result in a totally different pattern of outcome, that outcome could be emergent. When you tweak the variables that go into baking a cake, however, a cake will probably still result. You'd have to really screw things up to not produce a cake of some variety. Whether it is something you can present to loved ones without offending them is another matter.

We've said enough on this so far. Let the idea filter through your mind as you read the rest of the book and think about the world (we like to think you're reading this while looking thoughtfully out a train or airplane window). It will become clearer.

FEEDBACK

Feedback is simple and important.

It is also just what it sounds like: You do something, someone reacts, then you react, then they react, then you react, and so on. Feedback also need not be bilateral: what you do can affect the world at large, which in turn affects you. Or it can be between a single person and a whole corporation.

The idea that a single person's actions can change the world does have some truth when those actions gradually spread between people and accumulate to a big effect. For now, we can be confident in saying that individuals responding to others generate feedback, to which we all continuously respond, all of which aggregates up to big social outcomes. This goes a long way toward explaining how things like fashion trends rise and plummet.

If the word "feedback" elicited in your mind a microphone screeching in a conference hall, you'd also be on the right track — interactions of different parts give rise to big events. In this case, the big event (screeching) is a bad one. Feedback is perfectly capable of producing good things, too, like confidence, wealth, or brand equity.

Feedback empowers marketers with an understanding of consequences. In the real world, connectedness means that the things we do affect other people, and these effects can multiply and magnify and amplify — and come right back to us. On the one hand, it can be frightening and awe-inspiring: a slightly misguided message could have terrible consequences. On the other hand, it can be awe-inspiring and wonderful: ideas can travel, behaviors can change, and we can produce outcomes that make everybody better off.

Finally, feedback in its colloquial usage is relevant: it means understanding how people are receiving your product. When you turn in a report and people comment on it, you then update your report accordingly. The same is true for your product or your marketing message. The trick for marketers is that, while feedback is important, it is not always obvious or easy to get. Internet reviews can be helpful, and so can phone calls and focus groups, but you simply cannot sit in everyone's living room and watch them try out your vacuum cleaner and then update your marketing based on their beliefs right there on the spot.

Instead, you have to approximate by observing behavior. As we outlined in the mind and social network chapters, if we know what goes into behaviors, we can understand more about why those behaviors came about. Then we can use that information to make inferences about feedback.

Agent-Based

Feedback is easy to understand in theory, important for performance in many ways, and hard — but not impossible — to measure in practice. In the last chapter we'll dig deep into agent-based modeling, which allows you to observe feedback more closely than most other analytical techniques currently can.

INTERDEPENDENCE

Interdependence, unsurprisingly, is the idea that everything is connected. You may already be thinking about its nice connection to the above two concepts of feedback and emergence. Indeed, they are all tightly related ideas.

Complex systems are often nested. We all depend on other people, both within our particular level of a nested complex system, and between levels. We depend on our immune systems (individual level), our neighbors (social network level), and our country (macro level). Because we depend on others, we are affected by others, and they by us.

SELF-ORGANIZATION

In complex systems order can arise without the influence of a central authority. Most people interact based on their own individual incentives, without a central controller or conductor telling them what to do.

Amazing levels of order can emerge in systems where there is self-organization: We can see pandemics of both ideas and diseases, we can see species keep their population levels in a natural balance, and we can see businesses form to satisfy needs and replace unnecessary or outdated ones.

Self-organization also means that when it comes to analyzing models of complex systems, we know that we cannot engineer our own results. Because agent-based models, for example, work without central authority, there is no way for us to be tempted to plug in outcomes that we want. It's the ultimate safety against accidentally influencing results. We couldn't even if we wanted to. The most we can do is intelligently set the values of our variables and click "run." What happens is not up to us. We simply cannot engineer it.

COMPLEXIFY

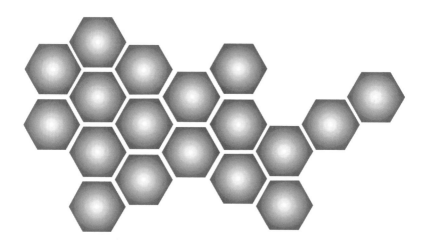

Complex systems are at once filled with many parts and yet simple. Emergent outcomes and patterns are simple and identifiable outcomes that come from the interaction of many parts. Just because there are many parts does not mean we cannot understand them. It just means we need to think carefully about how they interact and what each seeks to accomplish. If we know each actor's goals, and we have an idea about how they interact with others and the kind of network structure in which they live, we can go a long way toward thinking about the big, beautiful patterns their interactions might produce.

Sometimes complex systems do give rise to unfortunate things, like war, economic recession and epidemics. Other times they give rise to growth, health, and discovery. The work in complex systems is hard, but not impossible. Agent-based models are helpful in untangling them. We'll spend some time with ABMs in the last chapter. But before then, let's apply what we know about individuals, networks, and complex systems to some major aspects of marketing. Let's complexify things!

Read Further

Mitchell, Melanie. 2009. *Complexity: A Guided Tour.* Oxford University Press.

Page, Scott and Miller, John. 2007. *Complex Adaptive Systems: An Introduction to Computational Models of Social Life,* Princeton University Press.

Waldrop, M.Mitchell. 1992. *Complexity: The Emerging Science at the Edge of Order and Chaos.* Reed Business Information.

PART 2

AGENT-BASED MODELING APPLIED TO MARKETING

INTRODUCTION TO PART 2: NOTHING IS AS IT WAS

Actually, the world is basically the same, but how we think about it is changing. That, in turn, may indeed affect the world. In fact, we know it will.

We're going to spend the next several chapters considering how an agent-based modeling view of the world affects how we analyze the marketing environment, how we think about solutions to big questions in marketing, and how we attribute success and failures in marketing. The key points we'll be emphasizing are, first, that knowledge matters. By knowledge, we specifically mean it in the form of feedback that is both rapid and of high quality. We saw in Part 1 that the world is a dynamic place filled with fickle, often indecisive, and unpredictable people who are connected through an evolving social network. Given that premise, we hereby challenge you to try to make pinpoint predictions about future states of the world. Many people do attempt this very thing, and they run the risk of preparing for a future that may never transpire.

Instead, we are going to advocate that marketers (and everyone, actually – as we'll increasingly see, marketing has much in common with other aspects of social and business life, and all fields have much to gain by connecting insights) be prepared for the future, and be prepared to change.

Being prepared for the future is less about knowing the most likely outcome and more about knowing all possible outcomes. This allows for inclusion of unlikely events, extremely big events, small perturbations, and everything in between.

Being prepared to change means, first and foremost, setting oneself up for feedback. How do you know what future you are in if you don't have information about it? It also means being willing to change in light of that feedback. If you aren't willing or able to admit that you were wrong, that there is a better way, or that circumstances have changed, then there is no point in receiving feedback.

Okay, enough with the dire warnings. An agent-based modeling way of thinking means we get to consider more nuanced, subtle, rich, and dynamic processes and outcomes. This yields new insights to questions of brand equity, product development, competition, and more. We're excited to share them with you, and think you'll find you've been right all along — you just didn't know what to do about it (and in Chapter 10 we'll really tell you what to do).

Sales and the Emergence of Brand Equity

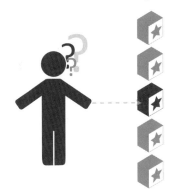

We can all think of brands we (think we) love: Nike, Scandinavian Air, Royal Jelly. We already said above that we don't actually know anything about love, and we stand by this claim. So, what we really mean when we say we "love" a brand is that, for right now, we have a mix of emotional and practical ideas that suggest to us a particular brand of a product is better than others. We might go to great lengths to acquire products of a certain brand, but even the most devout brand loyalist can be swayed to the other side by a better product by a better brand.

For example, many people have strong feelings about Coke or Pepsi, and we agree that the two taste different (we won't tell you which we prefer, unless one or the other company wishes to sponsor this book, in which case we like that one). We even have emotional attachments to our preferred brand — we remember great times with friends, outings to movies, and road trips that involved the brand. But if the other brand comes up with a flavor that is simply better than our current preferred brand, we'd probably switch to that brand. When push comes to shove (you know how those rowdy supermarkets are), we will pick the brand we want to drink right now when choosing from the selection on the shelf at the store.

Happy memories are great, and fondness need not necessarily go away. But those things don't buy products. Of course, as discussed in the mind chapter, these things do play a role in purchasing decisions — that still holds. Specifically, we might be less inclined to try a new brand because of our attachment to an old one, which would delay discovery that the new one is better. But if the new one is truly better, we may keep hearing from friends that the new one is good, and, per the power of the social network, will likely still at least try the new brand.

There's a more sinister version of the story to be told. We just told a happier one. Both products are great, but we simply are replacing a better one for one we still like. Brand loyalty can evaporate even more quickly if the brand's product starts to fall apart. This may not only cause you to switch more quickly to a new brand, but it may also strongly reduce your likelihood of ever going back to the original brand.

If you have a bad experience with a log cake from a bakery, you're not going to go back to try their stollen.

Yes, Brands Are Still Important

In this chapter we will describe a big insight that comes from a complexity science-based philosophy of marketing, and then offer five specific ways this insight changes how we think about and practice marketing. The insight is that brand equity is an emergent property of the complex system of the marketplace. It is not a permanent, concrete, or forever-reliable thing that exists in the world unlike a hard object we can hold in our hands. We can never say "now we have brand equity," and then sit back on our heels and enjoy the benefits.

Our five practical ways this insight changes how we study and execute marketing will be elaborated later in the chapter, but for now, we wish to emphasize that just because we cannot see or hold brand equity in our hands does not mean we can't learn about it and use it to our competitive advantage.

AN ABM VIEW OF BRANDS

It is an understatement that in marketing we spend a lot of time thinking about brands. Yet, there's no actual concrete thing that is "brand." Our goal in this chapter is to demonstrate that thinking about a brand as some actual, concrete thing is misguided. Instead, we think a much more useful way to think about brand is as a range of attributes, both tangible and intangible, that combine to create a temporary "perception" of a brand.

Arguing that brand does not exist in a concrete or tangible sense means that traditional measures of brand value — how much of that good feeling your customers associate with your brand, and how much they buy your product because of your brand over time also need updating. In this chapter we seek to demonstrate that a more productive way to think about brand equity and value is through a complex systems lens. This lens will also change the traditional concept of brand loyalty — devout adherence to a particular brand — so much so that you will want to make marketing decisions in a new way. But this doesn't mean brands don't matter anymore.

Whether customers develop ultimate acceptance — whether they buy a product based on a brand and develop brand loyalty for a long time — is an emergent phenomenon that comes about from the combined dynamics of the marketing environment that shape the customer's awareness and perception of the product. These marketing dynamics are in constant flux.

A point deserving special emphasis is that ABM views of brand equity and brand loyalty leverage separate measurements of brand equity and sales. You already know that sales and brand equity are not the same thing. Previously, however, we had to use sales as a proxy for brand equity, because brand equity was difficult to assign. With agent-based modeling, however, it is now possible to measure both sales and brand equity simultaneously and, more importantly, interactively.

Sales are how many people are choosing your product over competitors. Brand equity is how people perceive your brand. Perception encompasses the entire product experience, from initial awareness of the product through the flow of information gathering and social networking to the final decision to purchase the product, and the experience of using it afterward. Although a multifaceted process, if you can understand the mind, the social network, the mechanisms by which people influence one another, and how people change their minds, then you can analyze the brand experience and the value it creates.

As discussed in the section on the mind, customers don't simply know that brands exist. The brands to which customers assign value play a significant role in their lives and influence how they feel and act. Information about the brands is conveyed to customers through direct messages, information from peers, and product experience. In between and coloring all the messages are things like reputation, impressions, and emotion. It's not just what we see and hear — it's what we feel and experience that gives us ideas and opinions about brands. The resolve to purchase a brand comes after those ideas are formed and processed.

BRAND EQUITY AS EMERGENT VERSUS TRADITIONAL APPROACHES TO BRAND EQUITY

Traditional measures of brand value have been built from three static and discrete components: the financial performance of the firm producing the brand, sales and performance of the product, and an estimated version of brand equity that is derived from the leftovers of other performance measures. The leftover piece is often called brand strength, and is typically someone's best guess at how important the brand is to the product we sell.

In agent-based modeling views of marketing, brand equity is an emergent and latent property of events, updating, and interaction. Because of feedback and interdependence, brand equity can in turn influence sales. In short, it's possible to model out brand strength dynamically. Because it's embedded in the model, we don't even need to know the role of the brand or its historical strength. The model calculates brand equity continuously, dynamically, and organically while expressing it in terms of sales.

Specifically, complexity-based models of brand performance connect financial success with brand performance to dynamically calculate brand value. Because it is emergent, a brand's value is trackable and measurable over time. Interdependent variables like perception, awareness, and preferences operate alongside touchpoints and events containing messages about brands. These touchpoints can be anything from direct media messages to information from people in the social network, to experiencing the brand directly. Information from touchtpoints interacts with agent personalities, and agents update their views about brands to be higher or lower. Brand equity, the collective experience of how much brand influences purchase, emerges. It, too, can wax and wane, and it does so as an aggregate outcome of many agents updating their views and experiences over time. This will become clearer in the chapter on agent-based modeling.

FIVE LESSONS ABOUT BRAND EQUITY OVER TIME

We've spent a great deal of time in this chapter discussing how brand value is dynamic. Brand loyalty is ephemeral — brand exists in its own right and in a dynamic context. That said, we also agree that companies must have an accurate measurement of their brands' values if they want to define a successful business strategy. Even though they may not exist in a tangible sense, brands still play a central role in generating and sustaining the financial performance of many businesses. Most importantly, we need to know brand equity over time, especially since the number of brands continues to rise and diffuse values.

Earlier we introduced that the traditional measures of brand valuation do get us some way toward delineating ways brands create value. Specifically, we discussed how they do three things: They isolate the role the brand plays in decisions, they estimate how strong a brand is in its current condition, and they apply those metrics to a financial forecast. The result is a discounted cash flow and a net present value that does indeed depend on brand.

This approach lacks an important ability that a complexity approach can fill: the mainstream approach is not able to show how two important brand components interact, nor can it demonstrate how those interactions influence sales. To illustrate, consider the factory estimates of miles per gallon in a car. The estimates are not going to be consistent with real life driving experience because they never account for conditions on the road. Estimating brand value without on-going consideration of the conditions — the social, interactive, emotional, and economic context — gives you only a rough, and possibly very inaccurate, estimate of how much brand might matter on average. As we saw in the introduction, averages aren't the whole story. In fact, they can even mislead us.

A pre-agent-based modeling approach to understanding brands boils down to taking three independent measures and presenting them as a whole. Instead, we find it much more satisfying to evaluate how brand value emerges from the interaction of many variables that make up much of the brand experience. Specifically, we find agent-based brand valuation more satisfying for five reasons: it's holistic, it helps identify effective sources of value, it helps connect output values with the resources invested, it helps determine long-term ROI, and it differentiates between short-term and long-term equity.

A Holistic Approach

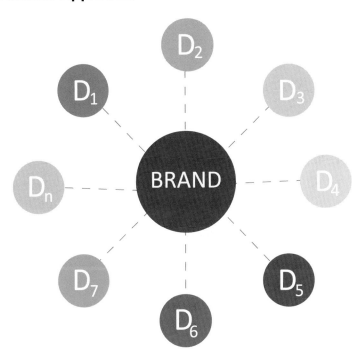

■ It takes a village to buy a box of cake mix.

Agent-based brand valuation that is built on agent-based modeling, along with other social science fields that study individuals and social networks, is able to take into account all components of a brand — from the people who experience it to the people who make it, and from the products themselves to their positions, partners, and producers (and other p-words)! Being able to incorporate all aspects of the brand and the brand experiences means being able to start to understand and even measure all of these tricky underlying and interactive factors that contribute to feelings customers have about brands. Think about it. Where do your feelings come from? We can all imagine that how we feel about something (our new bike) or someone (our childhood friend) has to do with a mix of many factors, from the advertisement we saw about our bike to our memory of playing freeze tag on a sandy lakeside beach. Feelings about people, places, and things come from lots of places, and blend all together with our personalities, knowledge, and memory to create big, broad perceptions about those things. There is no reason for a brand to be different.

Thus, a holistic approach to business and marketing is not just better for the sake of its being "holistic" and that of sounding like a desirable trait. Its holism actually makes it a more accurate measurer and predictor of brand performance. And because we can also include concrete elements like company sales performance in the mix, we can start to trace not just how changes in brand "feelings" come about, but also how they affect the company's sales performance. We can even tie new marketing strategies to positive changes in brand feeling — or negative. If your marketing campaign is not changing brand value for the better, that's valuable to know, too.

Sources of Value

| Word of Mouth | Product Usage | Online Behavior | Media Influence |

Figure 15:
Levers that Create Value

We saw that is it important to be able to evaluate whether your marketing campaign is contributing to improved brand value and "perceptions" about your brand. ABMs can do this by allowing for segmentation of activities, events, or behaviors, including, for example, word-of-mouth, product usage, online behavior, or media influence. Agent-based modeling holds as a big question something called "the assignment of credit" problem (Holland, see Read Further); this is a problem where, in complex systems, it is difficult to determine whom to blame or reward for outcomes.

The software we have developed doesn't perfectly erase this problem, but it helps us make more sense of our complex world. It allows you to splice up the many events and activities in people's lives, as well as the types of events you generate from your campaigns. Tracking them all closely improves our ability to determine to which effort to assign more credit. It helps you know which of your efforts are working. And knowing what worked and what didn't will make you a better strategic player in the future.

What's more, with ABMs you can even do this relatively quickly. You can run relatively straightforward model simulations that experiment with different levels of different types of effort, and you evaluate the changes immediately. Sales results become outcomes we, at last, really understand.

Connecting Resources Invested to Outputs

We rarely make just one investment, and we have many different ways of measuring outputs. How can we connect the resources we put in to the outputs we see? Again, it comes down to knowing what works and how.

All investments in products and advertising are bets about the best allocation of resources (we'll discuss the especially long-term bet on

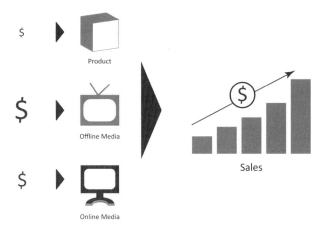

Figure 16:
Investment Levels and Sales

product development in greater detail in the next chapter). We can invest in a number of different marketing strategies and each one carries with it some expected return, about which we try to make as informed a guess as possible. Agent-based valuation can help us assess the impact of discrete or collected marketing campaigns (a method we call attributions). Again, because we can trace how any particular tweak to our strategy affects outcomes, we can determine which of our investments is giving us the biggest return, and we can better pinpoint our investments in the future.

Importantly, attribution is applicable to returns that are both tangible (sales) and intangible (brand value, loyalty, or equity). It's about perception, as always.

Finally, agent-based valuations also highlight how competitive decisions should be made to protect a brand — what makes it more resilient? It's one thing to be able to see how a particular resource invested can lead to higher returns in terms of brand value. But we also want to be able to push further and know how to make brand value last longer, outpace the competition, and be resistant to other changes in the environment, with our customers, and in their social networks. Again, because the agent-based modeling approach to marketing allows us to simulate all aspects of the market simultaneously, we can evaluate the effects of various changes elsewhere in our environment on the robustness of the value created by our smart investments.

Better Understanding Helps Us in the Short Term and the Long Term

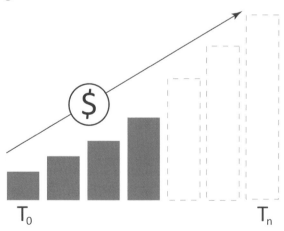

Figure 17:
Conceptual Framework for Brand Equity Management

Agent-based brand valuation can establish a long-term ROI metric, which can be used for monitoring the performance of your marketing campaign. Because ABMs allow us to be explicit about every single aspect that goes into a marketing campaign and every aspect we can think of (literally) that might affect the campaign or be affected by it, we can measure our brand against clearly identified performance targets. These targets and measures include everything from very soft measures, like consumer perceptions, to slightly firmer measures like awareness or word-of-mouth, to concrete measures like sales behavior. In short, ABMs allow us to be specific about our product, our customers, and the market, which allows us to set up specific targets to evaluate the performance of our brand. We can do this over a period of just one hour or one day, and we can do it over the long term.

All of this means we can identify opportunities. For example, we can ask and provide insight to serious, tough questions, such as: where can brand generate new revenue outside a core business? Does a brand extension make sense? In addition to helping reveal potential for growth, brand valuation, with the help of ABMs, allows us to identify risks. Does a promotion cost the brand too much equity? Will allocating resources away from driving current sales to changing future brand perceptions be worth it?

More Questions of Time: Short-Term Sales Versus Long-Term Equity

■ A carrot cake in the oven is worth three in the pan.

We swear this is a useful, if made up, expression. Actually, they're both valuable. A cake in the oven is delivering you benefits really soon, and having others standing by, ready to go, also matters. If you put too many in the oven at once, you have nothing for the future, but if you don't put any in the oven now, and leave them all on the counter, then you'll have nothing to eat for desert tonight. Plus, you'll probably also get ants.

There is an important tradeoff between short-term sales growth and long-term equity development. It could be the case that pushing efforts into one also spills over positively to the other, but often we have to make the difficult choice between investing in one or the other. The deep understanding that agent-based brand valuation provides can help us see the bigger picture. We can transform the marketing department from a cost center into a profit generator when we can connect brand investments with brand returns. Just because sales are up does not mean people are in love with our product. And people being in love with our product does not necessarily mean sales will go up.

For example, some people hate gas station coffee, but they keep buying it because they are cheap or because it's nearby and they are lazy. (Or both, you hypothetical cheap, lazy scoundrel!) This does not mean that the gas station is generating good long-term brand equity for its coffee. By a similar token, people may admire Swarovski crystal baseball mitts, but that does not necessarily mean they will buy them. Equity and sales are both important, but they are distinct. We like to think we can invest in both at once just by improving some aspect of our brand, but often we must choose one or the other.

Knowing the difference between these, simulating the differences in outcomes based on investments in one or both of these, and then attributing higher short-term sales or long-term equity to the original investment, all help us be wiser planners and marketers (and people).

THE VALUE OF AGENT-BASED BRAND VALUATION

To summarize, agent-based valuation offers a departure over standard methods of measuring brand value because it is holistic, which allows for comprehensive analysis of how many factors interact to create "value" for a brand. Because you can incorporate many factors, you can delineate the most effective and efficient way to outcompete hundreds of brands in a single product category. (We'll have some further thoughts on product categories and competition in the next chapters.) You can answer questions like: is it good to put all my resources into protecting my brand? If you learn that your brand is actually not delivering you much value, you may prefer to invest elsewhere — or change your image. Because an ABM approach combined with the workings of the mind in a connected social world means you can not only measure brand value, but you can also watch it evolve; you now have a fighting chance at knowing where your brand works and where it falls short.

Finally, the tradeoff between sales growth in the short run and brand value in the long run is at once subtle, important, and under-considered. Because traditional approaches to measuring brand value are linked tightly to non-brand-dependent forecasts of sales, we cannot evaluate the differences between short-term growth in sales and long-term performance of a brand.

Thinking about brand value in the context of agent-based modeling can help us be more forward looking. We can build simulations in agent-based models from data based on actual behavior of the brand, rather than static placeholders of behavior. Then we can run the simulations into the future and evaluate the effects of different dynamic settings year after year. Forward thinking, anticipating how a brand will perform, and being ready for changes can make the difference between a brand working for you and a brand not pulling its weight of investment.

If, in the course of your analysis of brand value, you discover the brand is not generating much return on investment, it may be time to re-evaluate other factors. For example, if a brand isn't working, maybe the product it stands for isn't working. It is to this we now turn.

Read Further

Perrier, Raymond and Stobart. Paul London. 1997. *Brand Valuation.* Interbrand.

Salinas, Gabriela. 2009. *The International Brand Valuation Manual: A complete overview and analysis of brand valuation techniques, methodologies, and applications.* Palgrave Macmillan

Winston, Wayne. 2009. *Financial Models Using Simulation and Optimization.* Palisades Corporation.

Feedback and Product Reality

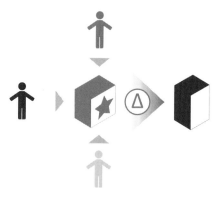

Remember that awful cake mix you bought that was all grainy and dry, and then baked into a hard, dense lump of flour and sugar? We don't either, and that's because all cakes are awesome.

Think about it: dense lump of flour and sugar? That sounds great. It is officially impossible to make terrible cakes, and this just might be one of the most important claims we'll make.

Other products aren't so fortunate: phones whose batteries die, cars that don't start, and shirts that rip immediately are almost never successful in the long term. We say "almost" because we firmly believe there is still a market somewhere out there for wearing ripped shirts in dead cars.

No matter what you say about your product, or how carefully you craft your marketing mixes, at the end of the day someone will try your product and form an impression of it. Research in psychology, which we'll discuss a bit more in a moment, suggests that once formed, impressions are usually hard to change. Depending on the impression, of course, this can be good or bad for your brand.

MARKETING VERSUS THE PRODUCT

A good advertisement can sell a bad product one time. A great campaign can perhaps get away with it twice. A truly brilliant ad might actually convince people that the crappy product is desirable (see above about the ripped shirts and stalled cars). Barring those extreme outcomes, however, most of the strongest brand impressions can withstand a few rounds of lousy product experiences.

The bottom line is that the actual product you are selling should not be overlooked when you are crafting your marketing campaign. Marketing, as you know, is about sending messages, and a product sends many messages to your customers that ads cannot. Agent-based modeling, combined with insights from psychology and sociology, can help us learn about how to incorporate our product with our message, craft our message carefully, and think about how best to allocate resources into product development as we look to the future.

In this chapter we make three main points. First, the reality of your product is that it is part your marketing campaign and part your brand. You can't escape it. At the end of the day we are selling things. We need to know what those things are, how they affect sales, and whether we should invest in improving or changing them. We also really like the use of reality here. It's one of the few moments we get to speak of something tangible — unlike feelings and perceptions and brand equity. Perhaps you can even hold your product in your hands. It's a nice grounding feeling. We're selling things.

In the end, you can make all the changes to your marketing campaign that you want, and a lousy product can still possibly pull it down. Later we'll discuss the importance of thinking about marketing in terms of the reality of your product, as well as describe how complexity can help us find a good balance between your product message and the product itself. What is the right gap between the message and the product? When should you turn up the message or tone it down? When should you invest in product development?

The second major point is that developing products means making long-term bets about the future. Media messages and marketing campaigns are also bets — you invest a lot of money into something with the expectation it will return increases over your investment — but they are far more short term. Think of advanced technology and medicine today. The products we see are the result of investments in those products decades ago. Even if you are selling something as simple as a cake mix (which, as we saw in Chapter 2, is hardly simple), investing money today in better recipes or new types of cakes means making a bet about a future that could be very far off. The more you know about your customers and how they operate, the more information you have at your fingertips to make informed bets for the future.

The third and final point is feedback. The more you know about your customers and their world, as well as how they experience your product, the better bets you can make. A complexity view of the world means that while the future cannot be perfectly known, we can be prepared for it. And we want to position ourselves so we can react quickly. You can't just sink money into a product and hope for the best. You need to have ways of getting responses from people who buy the product, and from people who do not. You also need to be able to use that feedback. Information to which you cannot react is not information at all.

We'll talk about this last point in the final chapter on consensus building. For now, we wish to emphasize that if you don't know how your product is performing, you cannot improve it effectively. And because you cannot be in the minds of every consumer, as mentioned previously, being able to use simulations for inferences about your product's effects on customers can be a great alternative.

NOT TOO MUCH, NOT TOO LITTLE.
(OR THE GOLDILOCKS OF MARKETING)

Because this is a book about marketing, it may seem odd that we are spending time on the product itself. In fact, the product is a part of the marketing mix. Broadly speaking, marketing is about sending signals to customers that resonate with their ideas and feelings in a way that drives them to purchase a product. Along the way, they, too, can become conveyors of information in their networks. The product itself sends many messages that will inform future buying decisions. Sometimes the product can be much more powerful than other advertisements or messages. Other times it's the reverse.

Either way, to imagine that crafting a successful marketing campaign is an art and science to be conducted apart from the reality of the product is to miss a great deal of the relevant picture.

We saw above that the product is a focal point — an anchor in a sea of possible beliefs about the product. It's easy enough to see that if you're selling a car, don't advertise it as a donkey or a flying car, as that will completely thwart impressions of your product beyond any useful extent. But what is the right amount of stretching from the actual reality of your product? While we like to think we are not encouraging dishonesty, you probably also don't want to advertise your product exactly as is:

> **"This cake mix will produce a cake that tastes exactly like all the others in a very average and more or less predictable way."**

There is a delicate dance between delivering a really strong message about a product and delivering a message that raises expectations too high. Some treatments of marketing give the impression that with just the right tweaking of a campaign, marketers can make people believe anything.

Here, we wish to ground things a bit. You can make people believe anything within a range, and that range is centered on the cold, hard reality of that which you are selling: your product. Think of it as an anchor in a sea of impressions — where your product falls in terms of quality is the space from which you work. Great advertising campaigns (actually, particularly terrible ones, too) allow you to stretch the range of beliefs away from the anchor, but you can never really move to a brand new, faraway spot without moving the anchor — that is, changing your product.

When an individual interacts with a product or service, an impression is formed, which is filed in one's memory for later use. You may be pleasantly surprised, you may find the product or service meets your expectations, or you may be disappointed. Whatever your impression, the effects are twofold. First, the impression formed increases or decreases the likelihood that you will consider purchasing the product or service again. Due to what psychologists and cognitive scientists refer to as confirmation bias, it's also often the case that repeated experiences with the product will cause you to further cement your original beliefs, rather than update them piecemeal in an accurate reflection to the product quality.

Second, the impression formed from your experience can positively or negatively sway the likelihood that individuals in your social network will seek out the product or service. This is because you may share your experience through direct (e.g., verbal or social media) communication, or abstain from purchasing or publicly using the product, which also gives impressions to others about its quality.

This means that each product sale is an opportunity for brand perceptions to shift up or down, for both the buyer, and for others in the buyer's network (and even for others' perceptions many degrees away).

PRODUCT REALITY, PRODUCT GRAVITY, AND CAKES ON FIRE

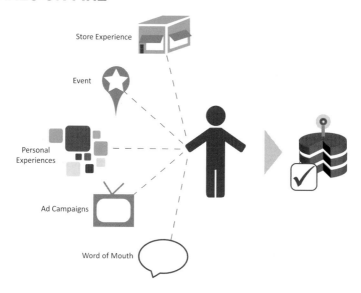

Figure 18:
A Marketing Ecosystem for Cakes

Product reality is more than just what your product looks like or what it does. The way a consumer experiences a product has to do not just with the product itself, but also with the context within which he experiences the product. What do customers need in the context in which they live? If the context changes, the existing feature set of your product will not match their use requirement. We don't care how awesome your flaming cake is, we just don't need it (unless, as we've said, you can convince us otherwise).

Earlier in this chapter, we discussed the idea that almost all aspects of marketing involve making bets about the allocation of scarce resources. Product development is the longest-term bet you can make. No longer-term focal point exists in a market than the product itself. It can take years, decades, or more to get a product just right. Betty Crocker didn't just roll out one cake and call it done. Allocating resources today, however, for a development of a product that will come out even as near term as one year from now means that you need to have some expectation about how it will be received by customers in an unknown and evolving media and social context.

The more adept a marketing manager is at planning for and understanding the myriad underlying social forces and consumer touchpoints surrounding demand for a given product, the greater his or her ability to build and protect brand equity. Because the finished product that appears on the shelf in a store is the long-term physical resolution of a bet by a company, the product decision is one of the most important choices you can make. You can take down an ineffective marketing campaign far more quickly than you can reverse years of labor and engineering that goes into creating a finished product. There is a manifest destiny to all products.

When thinking about marketing from a complex systems perspective, we can consider the product itself as a punctuation mark in an ebb and flow of poetry or song that is the part of the rest of the consumer experience, journey, or context. In some ways this is reassuring: at last, you can pin something down. It's a real, concrete thing that sits on a counter, in a stove, or on a platter with candles and frosting.

Once you've made the long-term bet, invested your resources, and now your product is sitting on shelves, you need to know how, when, and to what extent to change your product. Feedback is key to knowing when to change your bet. Feedback is simply information about how customers view your product, whether it satisfies their needs, and what would induce them to buy more of it. If you could convince everyone to celebrate the half birthday, you'd sell twice as many birthday cakes. Or you could just improve your cake so people want to buy it even when it's not their birthday.

The more you know now about how things are likely to be, the better the long-term bet that you can make in your product development. Most readers already know that it's important to get feedback — we seek it everywhere, and not just in marketing. Feedback in a complex system, however, looks a little different. Information in complex systems can come from lots of different places; it can be subtle, indirect, or direct, and it won't always give a clear indication of what to do next.

We cannot emphasize enough that the way to understand and anticipate the attribute requirements of your future customers is to know exactly what they want and why. In a complex system, what they want can change, and the closer your finger is to the pulse of what they want, the sooner you will know what to do.

A BET ON WHAT CUSTOMERS WANT

On one hand, this focus on the product gives us a moment of calm: It's a real, hard thing to hold in our hands. But it's also, for the same reason, completely terrifying. Get your product wrong (they don't want Funfetti??), and not only have you used resources, time, and human intelligence incorrectly, but now you are faced with the uphill and long-term task of developing a better product, and hoping that you get it right the next time around.

In marketing, and plenty of other domains for that matter, we shouldn't need to resort to "hoping" we'll get it right. We shouldn't have to believe that a product will be effective or will resonate with customers. We should know.

It is already clear from earlier chapters that an individual's social network is a significant contributing factor behind what customers want. And, of course, how humans make sense of the world —

through categories, emotional reactions, beliefs, memories, and more — tempers how customers react to new information, be it from the network or from the marketer or from the product. What's going on in the mind can drive really different outcomes from similar products. A slightly less than average product might cause someone who favors your brand to only be mildly disappointed but still generally positive, but it might move a neutral person to a position of negativity. And if many people already have negative views of a product, a bad product experience might drive all of their perceptions so low that they become extremely unlikely to ever try the product again.

Figure 19:
Key Influences on Consumer Brand Perceptions

Knowing your customers, how they respond to their world, their peers, your product, and your competitors' products is one important step. The other arguably more important step in a complex world is knowing how all four elements are connected, how information flows between them, and how those flows give rise to change.

Being ready for change means having feedback about as many of the four elements (consumer, peers, product, and competitors) as possible. The more frequently you get it, the more accurate it is. And the true power lies in the immediacy with which you get it following change. That's how you stay ahead of everyone else.

We have spent a lot of time emphasizing the importance of the product. It is important, but context also matters. There's product quality in an objective sense, to be sure (how fast does it go? How much weight can it bear?), but there are as many potential subjective senses as there are people in the world. Is this product good enough for me? Is it doing what I want? Am I sorry I bought it?

Or if you prefer: this cake is moist. But is it moist enough? A time-honored question, indeed.

Finally, another reminder: messages from brands themselves can affect what customers want. Therefore, of course, product reality is just one part of the marketing campaign you conduct. It's usually a more durable part, but it still exists in concert with all the other currents of life that affect what humans want.

Wait! One more thing. We've spent a lot of time here discussing being ready to react. Other times, it's important to take charge. Make a bold move, take a risk, do something big with your product without just sitting back and letting your customers tell you what to do. There is room for this — it's all part of the dance — and we discuss that in Chapters 8 and 9 on prediction and experimenting.

FEEDBACK AND THE LONG TERM

Products that test well in a focus group may not win in the market if the system dynamic is not fully understood. This is where feedback comes in. ABM can be helpful with understanding both long-term and short-term outcomes. Knowing things like how sensitive the success of your product will be to changes in the system dynamic over time can become a road map when it comes to product development.

In the short term, all marketers are limited in some way by the quality of their product. You can have the best media mix campaign in the universe, but you know deep down just how good your product is, and that will limit the ultimate success of your brand. Feedback from product users can help you improve your product — or decide whether investments in improvements are the wisest path.

In the long term, the reality of the finished product does not need be a boundary. It is a longer-term bet, but it is still a bet that can be changed. When you plan your brand over time, agent-based modeling can help guide your choices so that you use the very reality of your product in a way that shapes consumer preferences and perceptions just as much as your marketing campaign does. We'll discuss this idea further in the chapter on competition, but for now, remember this: your product is itself information to your customer, and the more you know about your customer, the more you can target that information to their needs. It's what they want, and it's what you want.

To summarize, your product is part of your message, and you want to know how it affects people so that you know where to allocate resources. Complex systems run off feedback, and getting your finger on that pulse is critical to being able to make a good bet against a dynamic world, a hard-to-predict future, and emergent outcomes.

Read Further

Davidson, William R. 1990. *Planning Premises and Strategic Alternatives.* Management Horizons.

Kotler, Phillip 2005. *Marketing Management.* New York: Alfred A. Prentice Hall College Division.

CHAPTER SEVEN

Interdependence and the Marketplace

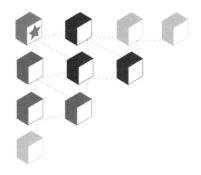

O h, alas, and alack, it is not enough to get things right. It turns out that no matter what we do or where we are, short of a vacuum in outer space (and even then it's questionable), we rely on other people for survival. But it's a little trickier than that: while we need others, we also compete with them for resources. We need other companies to provide complementary goods to help our product make sense (our frosting company would go out of business without your cake company! Imagine a future where there is no cake: We'd either have to eat frosting from the jar, or use it to make candy houses, or simply throw them all to the bottom of the sea).

But we digress. Let's talk about Evolutionary Fitness.

Survival in the market is about evolutionary fitness. The strongest, the fastest, the most agile — that's who wins. Biological principles dictate that this is true in nature. It's also the case in the marketplace.

You already know that if you want to succeed as a brand, you cannot just focus on yourself. Thinking about how to improve only your product, only your message, or only your media mix is not enough. You can perfect your message or your product, but unless you pay attention to the environment, which includes your competition, you can be left behind. If you are doing well in the market, you can rest assured that your competition will make it their number one goal to beat you.

It's a nice idea to think that we have to be constantly evolving, but who can in reality? Please feel free to imagine here an advertisement of a busy thirty-something looking up from her Smartphone in exasperation and sighing, "With my busy schedule, I don't have time to be constantly evolving."

In reality, this pretend advertisement is not far off. We really do have one million things to worry about all the time, and, for many people, we're lucky just to be ahead of our inboxes, much less constantly on the cusp of all marketing strategies currently and close to being employed by all possible competitors. The landscape is indeed complex. How can companies, or even merely marketing departments within companies, keep up?

There is not an easy answer to this question, but there is an answer. It is a complex one. (Are you surprised? If you are, you should probably put this book down and probably have a nap or something. It's important to take care of yourself, you know.)

The bottom line is: with the techniques for thinking in new ways and the tools afforded us to do so by agent-based modeling, we can begin to conceive of a world where we can anticipate our competitors' future moves. We can't know the future perfectly, but we can be ready for it. We'll talk a little more about the future in the future — more specifically, in the next chapter.

AN ABM LENS ON COMPETITION IN MARKETING

Here are five insights that an agent-based modeling view of marketing can contribute to our understanding of competition. Each of these points merits much more attention, and we invite enterprising readers to consider exploring many of these points on their own.

Market Boundaries Are Illusionary

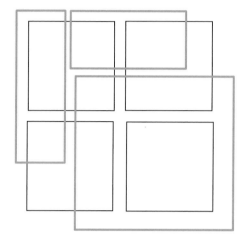

This first point is about how categories are important, but they are not permanent by any means. As discussed in the categories section in the mind chapter, all humans draw boxes around environments because it's all we can do. We have to make sense of the world somehow, and people tend to do it by putting things in different categories. They can be arbitrary, to be sure, but they often are well informed and reasoned. We put apples and oranges in the same category for a perfectly good reason. That said, there are other perfectly good categories we could use. We could sort apples into a group with flour and sugar (apple cake category), and oranges could go with bergamot, grapefruit, lavender, and eucalyptus (scents of hand soap category). Or if we were an 8-year-old at a Halloween party, perhaps we would put them in a category with pears, to complete the "Things for Which You Can Bob" category (you've never been pear bobbing?). Or if we were at a county fair, we could put them in a category with bananas as "Things to Put on a Stick and Coat with Something Sweet and Optional Nuts."

The important thing here is not just that it's fun to make up categories. In addition to being fun, thinking creatively about new categories can be a real recipe for competitive success. It can be a great way to innovate, appeal to a new market segment, change how people evaluate your product, and, importantly, evaluate it compared to your competitors' product.

When devising a brand strategy against a set of competitors, you do need to limit the brands and attributes included in the strategy. This is simply due to resource constraints, both in money you can spend and in attention customers can pay to messages. We can't just change categories all the time — it's exhausting. But we can do it wisely, creatively, and boldly. By highlighting the assets they believe strengthen the brand, marketers set the initial conditions of their category. Category boundaries are seductive and dangerous.

First, they create a false sense of security. Many times the existing market boundary can be exceedingly powerful and difficult to transcend. People's beliefs and communication with one another can strengthen perceptions to become quite solid. That said, changing boundaries is by no means impossible. It may be well worth it for marketing managers to put energy into reassessing the strategic set within which they operate. Rather than change your product, change how people consider it. A cake belongs in a category alongside other old-fashioned desserts for children, but what if you cast a cupcake (practically the same product) as a fun treat for a modern and cosmopolitan adult?

Second, they limit the marketer's imagination. To confine yourself to existing market boundaries is to wear blinders to tremendous opportunity, as well as to put yourself at risk of falling behind or getting trapped. Population, economic, technological, and competitive dynamics all create shifts which demonstrate that over-reliance on initial conditions can lead to failure. Continual evaluation of market limits is not only a source of defense but is also an opportunity for innovation. Testing these boundaries should be as frequent for brand marketers as it is for teenagers to challenge their parents.

Remember you are in a box. Your product and brand exist in a context that is rich with social, psychological, emotional, and practical considerations, all of which interact in ways that create outcomes that ebb and flow. How you conceive of the delivery of your brand is only as fixed as you allow it to be. Complexity can help you think about what the effects of pushing market limits might be.

You just might stumble on something that resonates with customers in a really powerful way, but you won't know unless you try, and you won't try unless you're open to it. Of course, as with any strategy, there is a danger that changing boundaries leads to negative results, but the more you know about your market, your brand, and your customers, the less likely it is you'll go wrong.

It's true, we need market boundaries in order to make sense of the world. But these boundaries are shifting, permeable, and malleable. We can influence how people make sense of the world.

In the spirit of competition, however, we hasten to remind you: others are reading this book, too, and thinking the same way now. So go ahead, turn on your imagination and rev up your agent-based model.

BRAND ASSETS DECAY

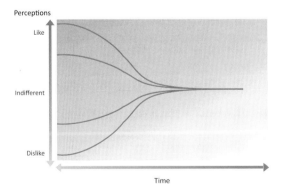

Figure 20:
Indifference and Brand Perceptions

Given a set of market boundaries and a defined set of brand assets, managers tend to overlook the rates at which brand assets decline. Decline is usually recognized in terms of extremes. For example, *Consumer Reports* might call the product a failure. Or a government agency reports a safety violation and a company must issue a recall. Or Jon Stewart ridicules an advertising campaign.

While each of the cases provides feedback to you about your brand, these results are extreme, and are often overemphasized both in terms of attention allocated to them and the reaction we craft in response.

Much more dangerous to brand marketers than these rare "big event" asset declines is the inevitable drift to indifference to specific owned assets that occurs for most brands. This happens when a brand's attendant attributes become neutral in the minds of customers. Their purchases are now vulnerable to someone else's campaign that can capture their attention.

When this happens, the work that these brand assets can do to attract purchases diminishes. The brand tends to become less productive. Neutral assets leak energy into the marketplace and are often overlooked because they are described as the "base" of the business. Delineating how the touchpoints of a brand contribute to the value that a brand creates is a must, especially for those assets that are the principal concern of management.

One of the many reasons brand marketers overlook the small yet sinister problem of indifference drift lies in a fallacy of the punctuated equilibrium. Punctuated equilibria are big moments when major parameters undergo shifts in value, disappear, or are replaced. What proceeds from there is considered a break from the past. These events are of obvious importance because they mean there is a new order around which we all must organize.

There are three big reasons why we shouldn't lend so much power to the big event that is the punctuated equilibrium. First, they are rare and in some cases cannot really be helped. We still cannot predict earthquakes accurately. Second, with the exception of big events that are disconnected from major social processes (like earthquakes), most big events are the culmination of many small events. A seemingly sudden tip from high brand awareness to brand indifference may just be the culmination of years of attention drift. Things can deflate just like that — but the deflation may have been years in the making.

Third, the reaction to the punctuated equilibrium moment is often misguided in its enormity. Because the outcome has changed so drastically, we may be falsely lured into a belief that making a huge change is the only way to revert back to the way things were. This is not necessarily so.

Be aware of this, pay attention to the long term, and be sensitive to small shifts. Your customers' attention is your most valuable asset.

Self-Organization Among Customers Is as Powerful as a Brand

The consumer is an active, not a passive, receiver of marketing messages. Like it or not, too many marketing approaches implicitly treat customers as pawns in a game instead of thoughtful players in it. If a consumer has a particular need that is not being satisfied by a particular product, they can conduct Internet searches, offer reviews, and communicate with product developers directly about their needs. Previously, customers had to find regional options for the product they wanted: we  were confined to our neighborhood grocer or baker for a cake. Now, customers can go on the Internet and actually (if they wanted to) review every single cake in the world. It is incredible that this is not an exaggeration.

With the rise of distributed information and the diversity of lifestyles, customers have increased their ability to structure their time and create new ways to learn about products. This empowerment means customers can be much more sophisticated about their needs, and they can do much more to satisfy them. Clear patterns of needs linked to personal effort create individualized customer purchase experiences.

Aggregated experiences are what we have described here as the customer journey. These customer journeys capture what is both relevant and differentiating.

It is popular to want to describe the current world as "new" and "different" from the past. In fact, it's almost trite. Indeed, there is novelty all around us, especially in the domain of communication. The major shift, however, is both bigger and subtler: no longer is competition about competing per se. The market is a co-evolving space as customers and marketers reset the balance of power. This close-in set of options is constantly being updated and must consider co-created brands from competitors as well.

Marketers need to plan their marketing strategies with awareness of this shift, and modify their organization to keep up. Competition is about information processing. If your organization is better able to process information about customers' needs than your competitors, simply put: you are winning.

You need to be better informed and informed more quickly. We simply cannot emphasize the importance of information processing speeds enough. It's truly the only way forward in the long term.

Specifically, connecting the customer journey to the brand assets you deploy is the only means of minimizing brand decay and accelerating brand equity. Knowing what touchpoints matter, the degree to which they matter, and what they must convey to customers will enable you as a brand marketer to efficiently allocate resources. The winning trifecta is a combination of media, investment, and message timed to the consumer aperture. By aperture, we mean that there is only a certain amount of information any consumer can process at any moment. Being there when the consumer is ready for your information is the key to your success, and knowing when the consumer is ready again boils down to information processing speeds that inform measured attribution — how much each part of the marketing plan contributes to sales.

The information flowing from the trifecta puts both the brand manager and the consumer on equal footing — a shift in dominance that reflects an evolutionary stability that has emerged for the first time in the consumer marketplace.

Every Market Has a Rhythm to Discover

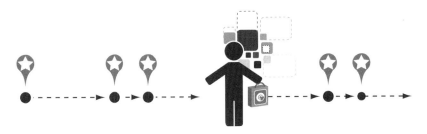

Figure 21:
Market Events and Consumer Aperture

People are buying products every second — every millisecond — of every day. Millions of birthday cakes alone are sold daily in the United States. If you are going to make a change in this millisecond marketplace, you need to pick some pretty fundamental things that are changing if you hope to make a difference.

What are the immediate events ☐ pre- and post-purchase ☐ that are bringing people closer to your brand? Now, zoom out from that: what happened the day before and after? The month or year preceding or following the purchase? Think about your own life: what happened between the last time you purchased a birthday card and now? This goes back again to the principle that the moment of purchasing is important, but it is still a moment in an entire lifetime. Many moments amass to fill the customer journey.

Return to the moment of purchase: what rises up in people's memories? The memory triggered when you see a birthday card or cake is going to impact your purchase.

As the customer journey and the brand marketer align (the moment the brand experience forms), both are influenced by the dynamics of the category in which the product exists. The level of involvement, the degree of emotional attachment, and the general word of mouth all influence the pace at which information is shared and processed. This information sharing creates the apertures along the customer journey that dictate when and what needs to be conveyed to make customers' perceptions more favorable so that they are more likely to buy.

While the conventional wisdom is that measuring these market events is impossible because they cannot be quantified (even this notion is breaking down), stressing the quantifiable over quality is not a best practice when developing competitive strategy. The ability to capture information from social media and online activities means that brand managers and customers are no longer separated from each other. However, to make the system work, both parties must be open to dual feedback — positive and negative. The consumer can tell managers what they need but the assumption that they are always right must go by the wayside as well.

This brings us back to a point from the previous principle: product development and brand experience are a co-evolutionary process. Old ways of finding out about consumer preferences, such as through surveys and focus groups, are still important, but they don't help us understand the two-way conversation that continually takes place between customers and brands. Again, it comes down to information: if I do something and you respond, the next time I do something I know about your response; thus, I can be more effective. Market rhythms change when your customers discover their needs are not being met by your product and go about seeking new solutions. Having your finger on this pulse is everything.

In short, this is not just about selling things to people. It's again about giving people what they want. Their wants and needs ebb and flow, and the great learning organizations will be the ones who survive — while adapting themselves to the needs of the marketplace — over the long haul.

All the actors in the brand experience are working with incomplete information. In the new paradigm of evolutionary stability, bringing all of this information into the light of day will solve problems but rightly erode asymmetrical power. Sharing the knowledge base will illuminate opportunities, adjust planning horizons, and create new pockets of time. All of these are key ingredients to overcoming the constraints inherent in the system. You can't know everything, but you can do the best you can with what you have. There is more information out there than you think.

Hierarchies Matter in a Networked World

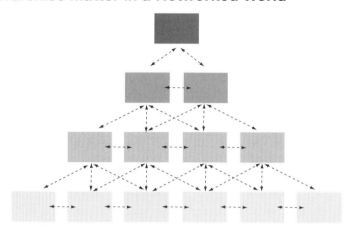

As the dynamics of the market accelerate through information sharing throughout the brand experience, both customers and marketers face ever-increasing numbers of shocks and deviations that cause them to reconsider their market boundaries. Brand strength — a brand's resilience — is the ability for the system to restore and repair itself after these changes occur.

■ The key is information flow.

Resilience for brand marketers stems not only from what they are trying to do, but who they actually are. Each brand has a state of being that reflects its competencies in areas such as research and development, marketing, human resources, and technology. Reflecting on these skills often drives managers to look at each capability individually. If this is all you do, you're selling yourself short.

Hierarchies can either help or hurt the flow of information within a corporation. We've said this before, but not in so many words: no one really knows exactly what he or she wants. Not your customers, not your brand executives, and not your marketing managers or competitors. The best a corporation can do is know why its product plays a role in someone's life. It's not enough to increase the flow of information from your customers to somewhere in your company. The information needs to flow throughout your organization. An insight that gets stuck in one small team is no insight at all.

Marketers should characterize their organization and its competition in terms of their overall function or societal purpose. This core mission is often overlooked — the least obvious part of the system, usually ill defined and seldom articulated. The absence of the feedback loop for employees, suppliers, and customers drives the "surprises," and the inability to recover from them. These hierarchies (the complete set of stakeholders) that fund the brand can overcome their self-generating constraints through awareness of themselves and the boundaries they set.

■ Remember boundaries? Please see above.

Read Further

Meadows, Donella. 2008. *Thinking in Systems: A Primer.* Chelsea Green Publishing.

Smith, John. 1982. *Evolution and the Theory of Games.* Cambridge University Press.

Diamond, Jared. 2011. *Collapse: How Societies Choose to Fail or Succeed.* Penguin.

Probabilities and Making Predictions

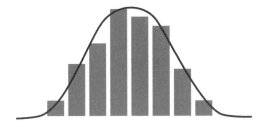

The idea of predictive marketing conjures in the mind the image of a crystal ball, a holy grail, a panacea, all three. We want to know what's coming, and we tell ourselves we just need to know a little more about this or that to be able to predict it accurately.

In an ABM of the world, predictions look a bit different. Because we know that small events can give rise to big events, that feedback can drive outcomes in unpredictable ways, and that emergence means macro-level effects may be surprising and by nature unpredictable, we are forced to temper our optimism when it comes to being able to pinpoint exactly what lies ahead.

This view is not necessarily limiting. If we change our focus away from looking for specific answers that might be wrong to looking for broader answers that are probably right, we can ready ourselves in new ways for what is to come. This need not replace conventional predictive analytics that forecast the future based on past patterns; rather, it can complement it.

In the quest for the holy grail of predictions, econometric firms have introduced models based on:

Fear	Am I going to do well in the future?
Uncertainty	What will the future look like?
Doubt	Is my model correct? Are my assumptions correct?
Deterministic analysis	Does my system correlate to yours?

Fear, uncertainty, and doubt are all present in many econometric models. These models, of course, do not always bring up these emotions, but these emotions are very often the inspiration for forecasting in the first place. Questions like the following are often (again, not always) present: Am I going to do well in the future? What if things go wrong? Do I have any confidence in my estimates? Are my assumptions wrong? How can I hedge against failure?

Many analytics firms have developed slightly different models based on:

A prior assumption	I'll just say all my observations are independent.
Utility	What do humans seek to increase?
Value	Where does my brand stand in terms of what people want?
Probabilistic analysis	What is the most likely outcome, and how likely is it?

An agent-based modeling view of predictions incorporates the features we've described in this book that point to the richness, interactive, patterned, and surprising outcomes we see in the real world. From ABM, we can instead build models based on:

Dynamics	Non-linearity
Probabilistic outcomes	Broad estimates

Sensitivity to initial conditions (it matters how today starts out), complexity thinking and ABMs encourage an approach to science that is based on confidence, curiosity, and creativity. ABM doesn't assume agents update in a limited, incremental, Bayesian way. It does consider human needs in a variety of different dimensions, including connectedness with others and emotional fondness for things. ABMs motivate exploration and testing of "what-if" scenarios. We don't need to worry about what will happen as much as we used to because we can run scenarios and see what unfolds. This of course is not a protection against bad things happening. It's just permission to find out what might.

The differences between agent-based modeling and regression analysis begin from the very setup of the model, continue through the means of analysis, and carry through to the final inferences from a predictive analysis.

With regression you are limited to your data sets — to what actually happened. There's no "what if" analysis in calculating a regression. And after you analyze what the data from the past tells you about what might happen in the future — should everything stay the same — you can begin to layer expectations onto what individually might occur.

With an ABM you start backwards from how a regression works. You begin by creating agents based on attributes you know about them and behaviors you know they exhibit. You form frameworks about what individual agents will do. Only after this do you input data. When we have a validated model, this means we think we have the causes of behavior right. It means the behavior of the agents is driving the outcomes in the system. Once we feel comfortable that we have the interactions correct, we can begin with "what if" scenario testing (more on this in the next chapter).

In short, there are two major benefits of the ABM approach. Again, we do not advocate an agent-based modeling view or an ABM approach as a replacement of more traditional models (or anything else that might be developed), we simply assert that the insights offered by ABMs are unmatched in other existing methods.

The first benefit is that its estimates are not just probabilistic, they are also nonlinear. Much of statistical analysis offers probabilistic estimates, but most models assume linearity. As discussed in Part 1, while linearity is certainly possible, it is not the only — and may even be a minority (but we defer to experts here) — principle by which outcomes arise. Estimating nonlinear outcomes from linear methods is inviting problems into your results.

Instead, when we use an ABM inspired by a complex systems philosophy, we are able to incorporate nonlinear relationships between variables, interaction between variables, and system dynamics. There is simply no room for system dynamics in a linear regression model; yet, it is clear they exist in the real world. One trick, of course, is determining when to employ which model. Again, this comes down to judgment.

The second benefit is that an agent-based model can offer individual and system precision. Although it can be uncomfortable, we need to accept that we cannot control or predict all outcomes. Other forms of marketing analytics do offer more accessible and familiar kinds of individual precision; econometrics offers comfort in the form of perceived precision as well. But the ABM should boost our confidence. It can help paint a broad picture that considers probabilities over all possible outcomes, and this can serve as a necessary complement to traditional forms of analysis that offer pinpoint forecasts based on past trends and assumed relationships between variables.

This is not to say ABMs don't make assumptions. For example, they assume certain relationships between variables as well as relationships between people (i.e., whether they are in a network and, if so, the structure of the network). In ABMs, however, every user has to be explicit about his/her assumptions. Nothing is built in.

The table below summarizes the major differences between ABM predictive modeling and more traditional regression-based predictions.

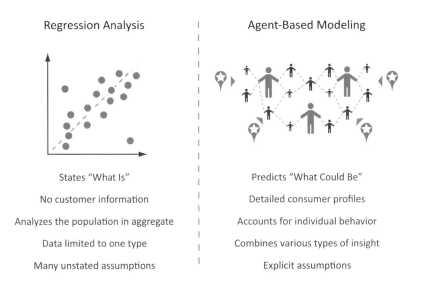

Regression Analysis	Agent-Based Modeling
States "What Is"	Predicts "What Could Be"
No customer information	Detailed consumer profiles
Analyzes the population in aggregate	Accounts for individual behavior
Data limited to one type	Combines various types of insight
Many unstated assumptions	Explicit assumptions

An agent-based modeling prediction offers a less precise solution that has greater explanatory power. It's a tradeoff. With the help of ABMs, we can watch outcomes grow and take place before our eyes — we can say how sales came to grow or shrink, or how equity rose and fell. But we cannot be foolhardy and enter in everything we think matters and hope the world comes out in an intelligible way. As we'll see in the ABM chapter, the best models involvemaking judgments to keep them representative and actionable all the way down to the individual level.

In a regression analysis you are given numbers after all the calculations take place. With an ABM, you watch a process unfold and see the results. How do you know it's true? Well, how do you know it rained? You watched it happened. And if you see something fishy happening — a process you know isn't accurate to real life — you can go back to the model and adjust your assumptions. Again, it comes back to this matter of the human element. We are measuring human processes and outcomes. And we need a human to think about the models. It comes down to the ability to judge. We're optimistic about the future, but for now, artificial intelligence just isn't there. (Between that and humor, we're staving off the robot apocalypse.)

JUDGMENT DOESN'T JUST MATTER, IT'S CENTRAL

The human element behind prediction and analysis is not to be underestimated, in either statistical analysis or agent-based modeling. If we do not allow judgment to play a role in the model, we are getting it wrong. We simply cannot automate everything. We are not alone in making this claim, of course. Many very smart people have thought long and hard about judgment in methodology and the limits of computation.

In the end, the three elements that matter most are: facts, rigor, and judgment. Smart data collection helps with the facts, models supply the rigor, and we supply the judgment. It's a human exercise. We're important.

FREEDOM

Agent-based modeling offers freedom from paralysis for marketers. We cannot know the future exactly, but we can predict possible outcomes and their associated probabilities. Predicting the future from a complexity standpoint means casting a light on all possible permutations to the system that could come from a single change today, given our parameters and assumptions. If we create a model that is an accurate representation of the real world, then we can find out the range of outcomes we might expect, as well as the likelihood of each outcome. Instead of saying, "Well, it looks like there should be an increase, but I don't really know how likely it is — or actually what would drive it," we can make statements like: "With 30 percent probability, sales will rise between 0.10 and 0.7 percent. With 20 percent probability, they will rise more than one percent. But there is a 50 percent chance things will remain the same."

Why can't statistical models tell us this? First, statistical models simply cannot capture the feedback and rich mental models that can be incorporated into models of complex systems. So they simply are missing out on major processes. Second, statistical models take an average of all effects. Averages, while helpful, are not necessarily very informative without knowing distributions over them. For example, learning that the average height of two people is five-foot- three tells you something about them, but not much. What if it is an NBA player and a child?

In most inferences we wish to make from models, the difference between an NBA player and a child is a big deal.

WE HAVE SEEN THE FUTURE AND IT IS...POSSIBLE

The mere fact that agent-based modeling allows for small events, large events, likely events, and everything in between means that if you have constructed your model with the appropriate inputs, you can predict the probability distributions over the likely market shares of your brand, sales rates, brand equity outcomes, and returns on investments.

In agent-based modeling, we are exchanging pinpoint accuracy for a broader view of feasible, dynamic, and interactive outcomes. We are providing population stability rather than statistical moments. Both are helpful.

But It's Not a Panacea

The predictions you can build from a complex systems model of the world are not a panacea. They do not offer instant, bite-sized solutions that you can pass through your organization tomorrow. You can get a lot more information from the outcomes of complex systems analysis, but on other hand, complex systems analysis and ABMs require a larger up-front commitment from the user in terms of time and thinking around the data inputs. Complex systems results are for mulling over, not flipping light switches (usually).

In addition, an insight that you might gain from an analysis of your market from a complex systems perspective may generate plenty of ideas for use in terms of strategic, long-term planning. When you use them, however, you will be modifying the system. If you begin with a set of circumstances, and then change those circumstances, the outcomes will be different. The mix of drivers and touchpoints that become optimal in the second scenario may not be the same variables that you originally found to be optimal.

These challenges only mean you need to be careful about your expectations when it comes to using complexity to answer your marketing questions. A complex systems inquiry into the world is not about getting the precise numbers to answer a specific research question. Rather, it is about constructing the big set of conditions that preserve or change your marketing experience and your brand success.

Once you have those, you can do much more than you ever could with the statistical models that use data from the past to predict average likely outcomes. Complexity lets you go right up to the starting line of today, cast a light forward and say: what's next?

Now, this light isn't going to be a big bright room. It's a penlight. But it's more than we've ever had before. It gets you to the starting line with the right initial conditions.

AN AID TO DECISION-MAKING

One of the major benefits of agent-based modeling analyses of marketing is that not just the results are useful. Complex systems analysis gives you some explanatory power over what happens. Simulating systems allows you to watch changes as they take place. You know when a television campaign strikes a chord in your population. You know among whom the chord strikes. You know by how much, and you know when it slows back down (if it slows down). Not only do we get the broad dual-cycle learning, but we have a tool that exposes all the things underneath it.

We believe agent-based modeling empowers the user to make better decisions in the long run.

We turn to these better decisions in the final chapter. In the next chapter, we consider exactly the kinds of analyses we can conduct with the aid of an ABM — including the testing of alternative scenarios and the testing of the viability of creative ideas. While there are ways to incorporate creative ideas — like a new marketing message — into a statistical model, they are cumbersome and approximate. With ABMs, we cannot get perfectly there, but we can get much closer.

Testing and Experimenting

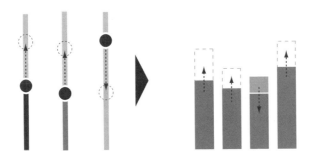

The dynamic properties of the marketing environment require a systemic interdependent framework to test marketing ideas. Agent-based modeling offers that. A prominent aspect of any ABM testing model is a feedback loop — actions from the parts affecting the whole, which in turn affects the parts. Incorporating this into any model that tests ideas and experiments with innovative ideas allows the modeler to evaluate not just the one-time effects of a change to the system, but also the broader, system level, reverberating effects of any change.

Feedback can take the form of positive returns and diminishing returns. Positive returns mean that the more you introduce in the system, the more it produces. Effects grow over time. Diminishing returns mean effects shrink over time. A closely related concept is "returns to scale" — increasing returns mean that the return on your investment magnifies over time. Decreasing returns mean that the benefit from any investment shrinks with each period that passes.

In econometric models, you indeed can learn about returns on investment. If you spend $10, do you get $11 or $12 back? You can absolutely answer that question with an econometric model. But, there's more to it than that.

Recall from previous chapters that subtle things, such as weak ties in a network, can do a great deal of work in driving outcomes. Econometric models cannot account for this. In addition, in a world where weak ties, feedback, and emergence play a role, averages cease to be particularly meaningful. The average effect of the flow of information in a network is not very helpful if some sections of the population are never affected, while others are strongly affected. In statistical models where the mean is king, you may find that your market strategy has zero average effect.

What this does not tell you is that it could be that your marketing strategy has a strong effect in some segments of your population, while it might have negative effect in others. If you could discern this, you would know not to throw away your media campaign — just redirect it. Averages simply cannot tell you that.

What's more, even if you managed to determine that if you separate your populations you see more accurate effects — you still wouldn't know what interactions give rise to it. What if the success of your campaign hinged on particular interactions by particular people? Averages cannot tell you that, but an ABM built from a basis of networked agents can. ABMs can help you detect the changes in behavior that your campaign causes that lead to changes in outcomes. You can discern the source of the effects you see. And then you can learn from them and build from them.

Finally, there is a tendency in more traditional analyses to focus only on tangible investments and tangible returns in paid media. More investment in ads leads to more sales. But there are also plenty of intangible investments and benefits. Word of mouth is an obvious intangible benefit, and the feeling from the color on your product label is an intangible investment. Most often, tangible investments lead to intangible results, like feelings. And feelings are shockingly, impressively, and magically hard to shake.

When you make investments you may also do it through owned media. There is also earned media, such as attention in your social network. This is another kind of intangible benefit of investment. ABMs can help you anticipate those. In the end, investment is about more than just money. It's also about time and content. And all of these, tangible or not, can offer increasing or decreasing returns.

TESTING YOUR IDEAS

Launching a campaign that is backed by in-market research poses two critical problems: a) this is an expensive, long-term strategy, and b)should the campaign fail to resonate with customers, the campaign may negatively impact brand equity.

The value of ABMs is that they allow marketers to test scenarios and plan for the action or inaction of competitors in a risk-free and easily modifiable manner.

Many innovations are the results of errors. These errors either tell us what not to do or, in some cases, they prove to be far more successful than ever imagined. Unfortunately, many errors are so costly that we cannot afford the luxury of making them.

Agent-based models offer a way around the cost of errors. Of course, as we saw in the previous chapter, ABMs are by no means perfect when it comes to predicting what will happen. But they offer a tremendous step forward in forecasting how interactions and feedback in complex systems will play out. Before the computational power of ABMs, our ability to do this was located somewhere in the range between extraordinarily difficult and downright impossible.

Now we can do it at basically the lowest risk imaginable. (Unless you're especially worried about carpal tunnel — but even that is a low risk here!)

What If?

You can test almost any scenario you can think of. The openness of ABMs means you can experiment on almost anything related to your marketing strategy, your brand, your product, your customers, and your customers' interactions.

One of the reasons experimentation is so accessible in ABMs is the free will of the agents in the models. Agents in ABMs are goal seeking: they have needs they wish to satisfy. ABMs allow you to test your creative marketing ideas against this backdrop. You need very little in the way of prior knowledge and other a priori assumptions about agents. Because they are already a self-contained system, you can manipulate the agents in any way you want — just as if you were in a chemistry lab and your potential customers were in the Petri dish.

CHARACTERIZE SOMETHING SLIPPERY: AN IDEA

Against the backdrop of free-willed agents pursuing their own micro-incentives, you can carry out your experiments. You can characterize your new ideas in a number of easy, different ways, which gives rise to a lot of opportunities for new decisions that are made in a new way.

Assess the Results of Varying Your Messages

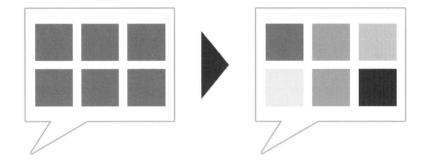

You might wish to change the quality of your creative. Do you need to put a lot of your budget into developing a really good radio ad, or will simply mentioning the product do the trick? Or perhaps you might experiment with different timing of your message or medium during your campaign. If you roll out your radio campaign first, and then your television campaign, does it make a difference in changing brand awareness, perceptions, and ultimately the purchasing behavior of the agents? You will not only be able to see the change in sales but also changes in brand equity for you and your competitors.

Measure the Sales Impact of Your Social Media Campaigns

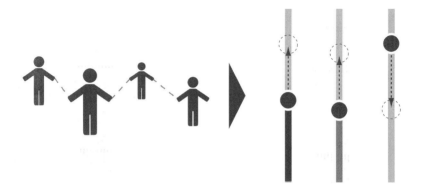

What if you change the touchpoints of your campaign within the community to which you target your campaigns. To give just a few examples of the many possibilities here, you might test the success of your marketing idea in a group that has low levels of interaction compared to high levels. Or you might test the effect of changing the speed through which information travels in your network (by modifying the influence of agents and/or their propensities to talk, post, or read). Finally, you might test how your campaign performs in a target segment characterized by high existing brand awareness compared to a group where awareness is low. It may well turn out that your campaign is better suited (in terms of ROI) for a social network that does not already know much about your product.

Examine the Role of Social Interactions Between Customers

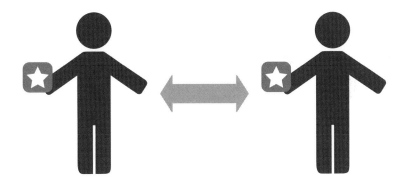

Third, you can characterize and test your marketing ideas by turning explicitly to the interaction between the groups you target and the message itself. What are the interaction effects of your message and the people in the network? What causes information to spread through the network? When does it stagnate? How does your message change depending on how much people talk? Does increased brand awareness translate into increased purchasing? Why or why not? Remember, because ABMs tell a story, it becomes possible to delve directly into answering the tough "how" questions.

Test New Media and Hard-to-Measure Types

Have you always used television to target your customers? What would be the effect of television plus direct mail? What if you add text messaging and skywriting? Test whatever you want.

Build Scenarios That Allow for the Probability of Small Events to Create Big Changes in Results

We have discussed the power of complexity and ABMs in accounting for large events and their role in the explanations of outcomes. Well, you can also account for really, really small events. Just a single person noticing an ad could make a big difference over time. In this way, small events can develop into big, emergent, unpredicted events.

See What it Takes to Go Viral, and What That Means for Your Brand

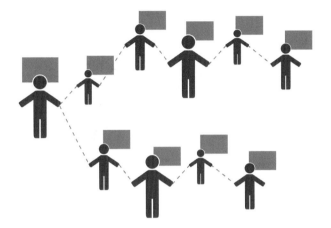

An example of a big event is a marketing campaign going viral, which is to say it spreads wildly through social networks. In many ways, going viral is a marketer's dream. ABMs can help you explore scenarios that will be more conducive to achieving such a phenomenon.

It is also possible that going viral means your marketing message becomes known far and wide, but the real question is: will that translate into purchasing behavior by customers? Not necessarily. Because an ABM can include both awareness of brands and the purchasing behavior of a brand – and because they can be included as separate, albeit related, concepts – you can examine how this might play out.

Explore New Product Developments, Marketing Scenarios, or Service Innovations Before Launch

Most marketers have mastered the fine art of developing product features and service innovations. Until now, it has been hard to forecast sales of those improvements with great accuracy. Most existing product testing looks to historical norms of similar products as a baseline for forecasting. These baselines take research insights on the new product and an estimate of sales is made. This approach not only excludes the impact of marketing but also overlooks social network influences that may lead to a breakthrough for a new product. ABMs overcome these limits and allow a better business case to be developed for new introductions long before they launch.

Test and Optimize Marketing Mix Options

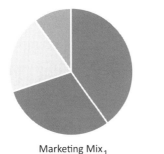
Marketing Mix$_1$

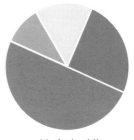
Marketing Mix$_n$

While traditional approaches to media mix look for equilibriums between marketing investments, ABM allows you to see how micro changes in your overall marketing approaches can lead to improved macro outcomes in your paid media ROI. ABMs help you connect the micro incentives of free-willed and self-interested agents to sales and brand equity change. What we do and what you do only matter a little bit in the grand scheme of things. But what we do, plus what you do, plus what nine million other people do — this can bring about surprising outcomes. Small changes in owned media, product experiences, and messaging can be tested for their interactions with traditional media mix.

If you're thinking that these macro outcomes sound emergent, you'd be right! So, it's true — the craze for Tickle-me-Elmos was indeed an emergent phenomenon.

Actually, this brings us to a much more subtle — and even sinister — point: even great outcomes for our brand in the short run may not be great things. For example, recall that we learned in the mind chapter that things are all too easily forgotten. A great burst of a campaign may stall out. Or causing others to be really enthusiastic about your brand could prompt them to also try your competitors' brands.

Every action has a reaction. Every outcome has an effect. These can be great, but they can also be dangerous. We can never predict the future perfectly, but our forecasts can help us be prepared — for both the good and the not so good. And knowing what not-so-good outcomes are possible can be even more helpful sometimes than knowing the good or average outcomes.

Pardon us for being trite, but it may indeed be true: with every shutting of a door there is an opening of a window. You may now feel free to stitch that on the throw pillow of your choice.

NOT MARKETING MIXES, MARKETING STRATEGIES

A final note: a marketing mix is more than what you spend where. It's more than just allocation of resources across various media types. It's a broad strategy — a comprehensive collection of paid, earned, and owned media. It stretches from the marketing message through word-of-mouth effects, the product reality, and the brand experience. With the ability to measure elusive concepts, test ideas, and analyze outcomes, you can now be creative, think outside the box, and shake things up — without fear of spending millions of dollars and six months of your life on something that disappoints.

OPTIMISM

We wish to impart a sense of optimism in the end. We can sequence what happens in marketing and understand the outcomes we see in ways we never could before. Of course, it's still not perfect, and we cannot make sweeping causal claims left and right. But we can offer a new way of thinking about and assessing outcomes in our analytical models. All models are hypotheses — they are expectations based on simplifications about how the world works. Many of the more traditional models do not allow us to incorporate things we believe about how the world works — like that there is feedback, or that we learn from our friends, or that no matter how low the price goes, we may not make a purchase without some shock.

The reason we are spending so much time on the virtues of ABM is because we believe it can change the world for the better. Getting at underlying processes, interactions, and the power of initial conditions to shape distant futures in a systematic way is revolutionary. It is a brand new way of analyzing how things happen in marketing. And we believe it echoes what we all believe is true — that random events can sometimes matter, and that little bits of influence here and there can lead to big changes.

Experimenting is not just blindly running trials into a deep, dark hole of a future that we cannot portend. Instead, it is about following a principled set of steps in evaluating likely scenarios of outcomes based on particular changes in an interconnected system. It's careful work, it requires judgment, it exists only if there is creativity, and it's just beginning to be recognized as a valuable approach to planning.

But it's not enough to just click the button on the model that says "run." Powerful results reward only those who spend the time to learn about how the underlying concepts and dynamics work. Knowing how network structure should affect the spread of information, or whether to look for emergence, or that perceptions change slowly over time, means that results from an ABM will be far more useful to you than someone who knows only to look for an increase in sales. In many ways, an increase in sales is the last thing one should look for. By then, it's already done. The sale is made. It's the process we care about. If you want to increase sales, don't increase sales in your model. Increase the ideas and behaviors that give rise to the decision to purchase. Sales — that's too late.

Our wish is for marketers to realize there is more to analysis than pulling levers and seeing controlled outcomes. Everything is connected. In this view, the idea that we can hold some aspect of the world constant while varying just the element about which we care (e.g., a new marketing campaign) starts to make less sense. Very little of the real world that we care about in marketing is things we can just hold constant at will — yet we regularly impose this constraint on our models. It is important to be aware of this, but awareness is not enough.

Ultimately, we will show you how to do something about all of these complexities and connections. Rather than just throw up our hands and say, "It depends," we can actually use insights from complexity to make predictions and develop better-informed courses of action. We become better analysts of social processes and outcomes not in spite of all the complexity in the world, but because of our recognition and understanding of it. To this end, the next chapter introduces you to agent-based modeling. In it, we'll discuss how ABMs can lead to better decision making and inspire more creative marketing ideas and, in turn, experimentation.

The next generation of thinking is a positive one. We can learn from ABMs what not to do, to be sure, but even more importantly we can learn what we can do. And we can act with less fear. All is under control. And by "control" we mean "self-organization." We can still pull levers, we just need to realize that the effects won't necessarily be straightforward, predictable, or easy to understand. And once we realize that, we can pull levers far more effectively. Time is of the essence, and so is correctness — even if at the expense of some accuracy.

Read Further

Schelling, Thomas C. 1978. *Micromotives and Macro Behavior.* New York: W. W.Norton & Company.

Gould, Stephen J. 1982. *"Punctuated Equilibrium: A Different Way of Seeing."* New Scientist 94, 138.

Gould, Stephen J. 2002. *The Structure of Evolutionary Theory.* Cambridge: Harvard University Press.

Our Agent-Based Model

W e've covered all of the necessary concepts. You know that how people are connected has huge implications for how information spreads between them. You know that tiny changes in marketing campaigns are capable of generating big effects. You know that understanding how people update their beliefs about products is crucial to forecasting purchasing behavior. And you know that product reality is not necessarily a trap but an opportunity.

But what do you do with all of this knowledge? How do you make sense of a world where everything is connected? This chapter presents the icing on the cake: the agent-based model driven by our software platform: Concentric ROI™.

INTRODUCTION TO AGENT-BASED MODELING

Agent-based modeling integrates several data sources. It provides very detailed results that cannot be achieved using other modeling techniques. ABMs are easily customizable, and they are flexible. Useful analysis is even possible when there is missing data.

This is the tool that will change how you think about, analyze, and interact with the world. Agent-based modeling is one method for analyzing complex systems. An agent-based model is at a very basic level a mathematical model where the focus is on individuals who not only act in specified ways, but also react and sometimes even adapt.

Most ABMs are computational, but they don't have to be. To illustrate a very simple ABM, consider one created by the famous social scientist Thomas Schelling in the 1960s.

He built the model and conducted the entire analysis with only pen and paper. Today we almost exclusively use computers, as our analyses tend to involve many variables and our questions tend to be more complex. That said, the simplicity of Schelling's model serves as a valuable example that you can learn a great deal even from the simplest model you can imagine.

EARLY AGENT-BASED MODELING

Schelling considered the effects of small changes in neighbors' preferences on levels of segregation in neighborhoods. He created a model to explain why we see such high levels of segregation. Do people really dislike people of other races as much as these high levels of segregation suggest?

Schelling answered his question by building a very simple and elegant ABM that simulated a neighborhood.

He built the model and conducted the entire analysis with only pen and paper. Today we almost exclusively use computers, as our analysis tend to involve many variables and our questions tend to be more complex. That said, the simplicity of Schelling's model serves as a valuable example that you can learn a great deal even from the simplest model you can imagine.

ABMs have several parts. Often, they are built on a physical landscape; common ones include grids or networks. They also consist of diverse agents who populate the landscape. These agents are given rules of behavior. This is the minimum requirement for an ABM to begin.

Schelling's setup was a grid — actually, very much like a checkerboard. It was intended to represent a neighborhood, where each square is a home, each piece is a family, and the colors black and white represent the race of a family.

The innovative idea in this model was that actors each made moves that depended on the behavior of other actors. And then, in turn, their actions affected the moves of other actors.

Specifically, the order of play was: each agent considered its neighbors and open places to move. If an agent were able to choose between moving to a spot nearer to more pieces of the same color, the agent would move. If no such move was possible, the agent remained in its position.

The results of the model were shocking. It turned out, with this setup only a very, very slight preference to live next to someone of the same race led to dramatic differences in where people decided to live.

Essentially, this example illustrates an important concept — emergence, which we have been discussing throughout this book; the aggregation of small individual behaviors can have large, macro outcomes.

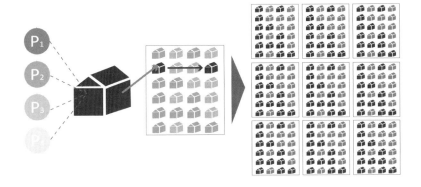

When we spoke of individuals in a social network, we saw how a message shared by one person could affect another person's behavior. We then saw how that person's behavior could affect yet another person's behavior. And many people's behavior affected more people's behavior and their awareness. One action had rippling, cascading effects through the whole system. Sometimes, actions can even come back to affect yourself.

■ What we do today affects what we do tomorrow — but not necessarily directly.

Interactions are the key to understanding complexity and are the foundation of all agent-based models. Because the elements in a model of a complex system, such as a marketing environment are so numerous, and each with its own set of interactions, the analysis almost always is conducted computationally. With advances in technology, these analyses can also be conducted rapidly using real-life data.

PRINCIPLES OF A GOOD ABM

There are several principles that help create a good ABM. The following three make up the grammar, or rules, for constructing ABMs.

Simple

There should be clear boundaries between what is included and what is excluded in the model. An ABM should contain just enough moving parts to be useful. We have spoken a

bit about sensitivity to initial conditions in many complex systems. One central means to simplicity is to think about the most important initial conditions to get the model running. It's less important to worry about what new variables to add, and more important to focus on being explicit about the variables we already know belong. We already have a million ideas about what might matter. Winnowing down what variables matter and being explicit about what they mean and what they look like is far more important (and difficult) than coming up with more and more examples of what might matter, in some cases.

That fact that ABMs force the analyst to be explicit in his/her assumptions is nothing short of a gift to all of us who wish to test the relationship between how we think about the world and how the world actually operates. You may be surprised to discover that once you make your assumptions explicit, they perhaps aren't quite on point. We all have beliefs about how the world works, and we usually look for evidence that confirms those beliefs (and when we can't find evidence to validate our assumptions, we are terribly good at bending results so they look like they fit). The act of making assumptions explicit and then seeing what they imply is a wonderful reality check for all of us. Is there a link between your view of the world and reality?

Once we know that our assumptions are accurate, we can start to adapt to the changing world with much greater success. Because it is possible to have unintended consequences from all purposeful actions, you cannot know what the ultimate outcomes will be. If you don't even know the actions or conditions to start with, it's hard to imagine you'll be anything but permanently lost in your analysis.

Being specific about initial conditions can also be helpful with collaboration. If you and your stakeholder can agree on the initial conditions and your assumed values, you know for sure you are beginning from the same point. Then you can systematically evaluate what happens.

Finally, being simple and specific is important for the general success of the model. If you begin with too many initial variables, it becomes difficult to isolate causes. Too few and the model may not only miss reality, but it may just stand still. As with statistical analysis, finding the sweet spot of the right number of variables to include is both a scientific and creative endeavor.

Experts in marketing will have a good idea of what the key pieces are that matter in a market. And again, the act of making the assumptions about basic components of the model is extremely instructive on its own.

Before we go on, you may be asking: isn't the point of the modeling exercise to find out what matters? Why am I responsible for putting these elements in myself?

Our answer is, first: being explicit is itself a more than worthy exercise. And second, ABMs face the same basic constraint that is faced by all matter in the universe: you can't create something from nothing. We have to start somewhere. Starting with the expertise of marketers, who know their market, product, and customers better than anyone, is hard to beat as a starting point.

That said, one additional way to leverage ABMs to generate insight might be to have people who are non-experts determine the basic moving parts. What an outsider thinks is important can sometimes not only be different, but it may be illuminating and, in some cases, offer surprising advances over the current expert knowledge.

When in doubt, if you have no idea what to put into your model, going with the average is a safe bet. If you're planning a marketing campaign where, hypothetically, bakeries in the U.S. are a relevant factor, you might just put in the average number of bakeries in an average-sized U.S. city.

One of the many especially useful aspects of ABMs is that once you have put in something like the number of bakeries in the model, you can parameterize that factor and in your analysis consider the differences in outcomes between scenarios where there are very few bakeries present versus where many bakeries are present. That will give you an idea of how sensitive (hey!!) the model is to you getting the number of bakeries correct. And if you are correct, it tells you something really helpful about how much you might worry if a whole bunch of new bakeries crops up in your prized sales regions.

Valid

While one of the most exciting aspects of ABMs is that they can generate surprising and unpredictable results, these unexpected results are only helpful to the extent that your ABM is accurately reflecting reality. An ABM is in fact only useful insofar as we believe with some confidence that the model is providing results based on a realistic depiction of how the world works.

This is actually very similar to statistical models: ABMs and statistical models both have elements that we should be able to look at, understand, and think, "Okay, this makes sense." Having established that some of the more predictable elements of the model are being produced in a fashion consistent with our own knowledge of the real world, we can then turn to other parts of the model that may surprise us.

There are a number of techniques available to examine the validity of an ABM. These range from simply looking at the results of the model and applying our own knowledge to evaluate the accuracy of the patterns generated to using data from the real world as a test of the accuracy.

More often than not, it is sufficient for at least the first steps of an analysis to simply look at the processes and outcomes of the model. Are the results for the aspects of the model about which you are already knowledgeable consistent with your expectations? If so, you can feel more confident in the validity of your model.

Useful

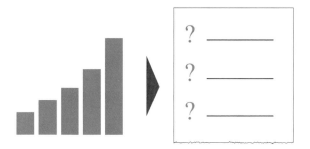

A model that is valid need not necessarily be useful, but a model that is not valid will automatically not be useful. Three aspects of validation include, first, validating assumptions. These are the things we build into the model that drive our outcomes. We want to use our understanding of the world — be it in the form of data or our best estimate — to set up a model that reflects the world. The second side is the validation of our outputs: we need to examine the outcomes and evaluate whether they are plausible given what we know about the world. If they are not, we return to our inputs: have we made assumptions that are not quite right? Examining the validity of outputs is itself a good test of the accuracy of our own mental models of the world.

A third aspect is sensitivity analysis and calibration. Depending on the absolute precision with which we want to pinpoint outcomes in the future, we may wish to calibrate the model up to thousands of times to get it as close to reality as possible. Other times, we may prefer broader assessments of general relationships between variables of interest, system dynamics, or the universe of possible outcomes at a general level. Both are useful; they are just different.

The point is that precision is not the same thing as validity or usefulness. Imprecise models can be very useful. Even incorrect models can be useful. We believe modeling is almost always a productive exercise. Again, this is not to say a model needs to generate profound results in order to be useful. A model that does not yield much in the way of insightful results is in itself a result: you have learned what is not important or effective. In fact, what you learn may even surprise you. Non-results may be less glamorous, but they are almost always instructive.

In addition, as described above, the mere exercise of building a model is almost always an educational experience in your subject. Determining what belongs in your simplification of the world, as well as how you will best conceptualize and measure it, requires that you think carefully and diligently. You may surprise yourself in what you come up with and how you prioritize it. Indeed, the act of crafting a model is often a surprisingly satisfying experience of joining your deep knowledge with your untapped creativity.

We are rarely given the gift of opportunity to apply such discipline to our thought in everyday considerations.

WHY USE ABMS?

The entire arc of ABM creation gives a marketing model exercise meaning in three ways:

Explain

ABMs tell a story. They give more than just a table of results. We can watch the process unfold and learn from it. At what point does brand equity increase? When do customers update their beliefs about a product most? By watching the story of the consumer's journey, we learn about our customers, our messages, and our products. This increased understanding of processes helps us explain outcomes that make us better off. And all of this helps us be better marketers — and better interpreters of the world around us.

Predict

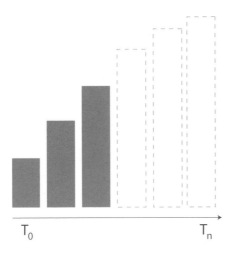

What's next? ABMs help us quantitatively enumerate the future. They help us less accurately predict more outcomes. Another way to put it is they help us predict ranges of outcomes while being sensitive to probabilities over those ranges. Most statistical predictions only collect those aspects of prediction into one specific point.

Empower

You are in charge of ABMs.
They're not in charge of you.

When you use ABMs to answer your
important questions, you are in the
driver's seat. You can test your new ideas and
you can compare existing strategies. You can
change any aspect of the model to satisfy your
curiosity. You use ABMs to empower you to
make good, informed, and pretested ideas. An ABM is a way of
practicing for the real world, enabling you to attack it more
confidently and better prepared than you would otherwise be.

LET'S MAKE A CAKE

We have developed an ABM that shows how you pragmatically apply
the concepts we have discussed to real-life marketing questions. For
this example, the brands we will analyze include the leading grocery-
store cake brands, Betty Crocker and Duncan Hines, and a third
brand that is a regional bakery, specializing in a variety of cakes
suitable for many occasions. We will define this market by four
attributes, or drivers, of purchase: the taste of the product (which we
will treat as an intangible driver given the subjective nature of this

attribute), the price of the cake, the texture of the cake, the convenience of purchasing the brand, and the value of the cake brand for celebrating a special occasion. We will also identify three consumer segments to analyze: Moms, Dads, and Singles.

To help illustrate the concepts, we have included screen shots from our proprietary ABM platform.

Figure 22: View of Category Settings

After establishing the brands, attributes/drivers of purchase, and consumer segments or stakeholders we would like to analyze in our model, the first step in building a model involves defining the category. In our baseline scenario, Betty Crocker and Duncan Hines have advantages over the regional bakery in terms of price, but the regional bakery has advantages in terms of convenience and variety of cakes for a special occasion. Therefore, in the objective "product" section of our model where we compare the relative merits of the brands, Betty Crocker and Duncan Hines receive higher scores for "price," and conversely lower scores on "convenience" and "special occasion." Data that informs this section of our model may include product specs, analyst reports, consumer reviews, or industry or financial analysis for the category under study.

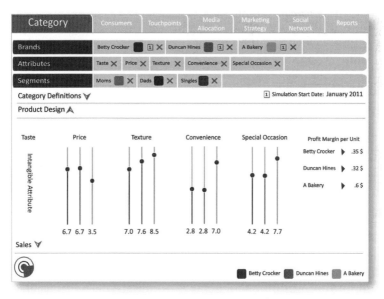

Figure 23: Settings for Product Realities

We will define the consumers in our model according to their behaviors, what is most important to them when considering the purchase of a cake, their awareness of the three brands we are analyzing (i.e., Betty Crocker, Duncan Hines, and a regional bakery), and their perceptions of these brands.

In our simulation, Moms represent a greater proportion of the total market, and they also do more of the purchasing of cakes. In terms of these groups' likelihood to discuss cakes in general, Moms are more likely to discuss cakes with individuals in their social network, but we assume all three segments have an equal likelihood to engage in online behavior, including reading about cakes and posting information online. Sociometric surveys or online social data typically informs the behavioral inputs in this section of the Concentric ROI model.

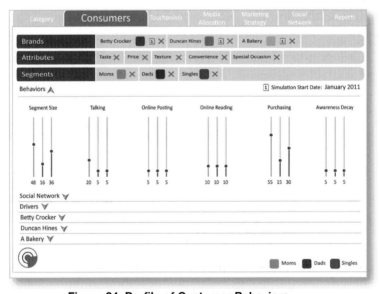

Figure 24: Profile of Customer Behaviors

Certain consumer segments may have a greater likelihood to be connected to other individuals in their social network, and they likely have varying degrees of influence on other segments. For this model, we assume Moms are the most connected consumer segment, and they have the greatest degree of influence over other Moms when considering the purchase of a cake. Dads, meanwhile, may influence Moms, but they have a greater level of influence on other Dads. For this simulation, we assume Singles exert influence over Moms and other Singles. This information informs our initial inputs for Connectivity and the Influence Matrix in our model.

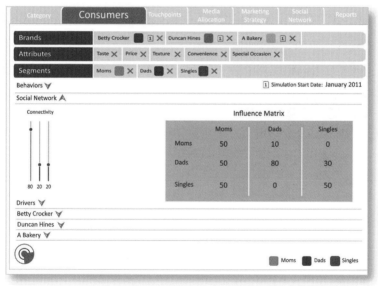

Figure 25: Social Network Influence

To complete our consumer profiles, we must define the level of awareness each segment has across the brands in our model, and consumers' perceptions of these brands at the start of the simulation. We assume individuals in all three consumer segments

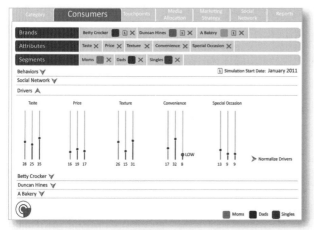

have a high awareness of the leading grocery store cake brands, Betty Crocker and Duncan Hines. Although awareness is much lower for the regional bakery (below 50% for all segments), Moms

Figure 26: Customer Preference Settings

and Singles are the most aware of this third alternative. Finally, how do Moms perceive Betty Crocker on its taste, price, texture, convenience, and value for a special occasion? For each brand and each segment, we define the perceptions across these drivers. Data for this piece of the model may come from a brand tracker,

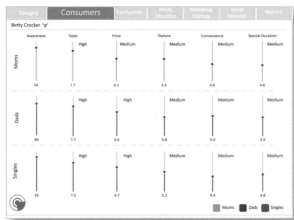

Figure 27: Sample Brand Perception

but qualitative insight or expert judgment is also sufficient to inform this piece of the model.

The next area of the model involves defining the touchpoints of the brands, including paid, owned, and earned media. For our model, we will define four paid touchpoints (i.e., the retail experience, advertising, digital, and CRM direct) and four owned touchpoints of the brands (i.e., YouTube, Twitter, Facebook, and the company website). We define earned media as online behavior, word-of-mouth, and usage of the products.

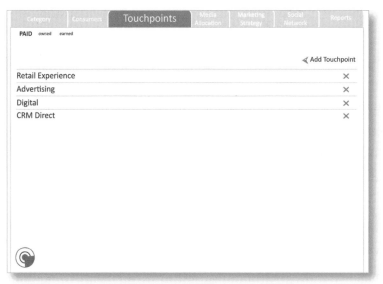

Figure 28: Basic Touchpoint Mapping

Econometric data typically informs the touchpoints section of the model. The effectiveness of a touchpoint is defined by its ability to

Figure 29: Performance Profile for Touchpoints

change a consumer's perception of the product in relation to the number of times a consumer must see the ad for his or her perception to change. Weekly and annual reach estimates for each touchpoint define the proportion of each consumer segment that will see the ad during the simulation. In our cake model, we assume the retail experience and advertising are the two most effective paid media channels in terms of their ability to alter consumer perceptions of the brands in our model. We also assume a greater percentage of Moms, Dads, and Singles will be exposed to the retail experience and Advertising for these cake brands on a weekly and annual basis, compared with the less effective paid touchpoint, digital and CRM direct.

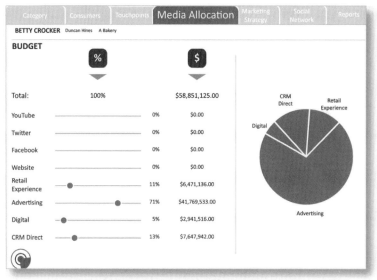

Figure 30: Media Mix Settings

Finally, we will incorporate the total media investment for each brand across these paid and owned touchpoints, as well as the timing of the marketing messages that occur during our simulation. In this model, Betty Crocker and Duncan Hines have the largest marketing budgets (both exceeding $50 million), with the majority of dollars allocated to advertising, followed by the retail experience, and CRM direct. Meanwhile, the regional bakery has a much smaller total marketing budget (i.e., approximately $12 million), with 95% of its budget allocated to advertising.

We will also define the quality of the creative for the different touchpoints of the brands, as well as the emphasis given to the different drivers of purchase (e.g., taste, price) in the creative campaigns for these brands. With respect to Betty Crocker's advertising campaign, we assume the company emphasizes the taste of its cakes, the low price, and the convenience of picking up a cake mix at the regional grocery store. We assume the quality of Betty Crocker's messaging around the great taste and low price of the brand are above average, while emphasis on convenience is below average.

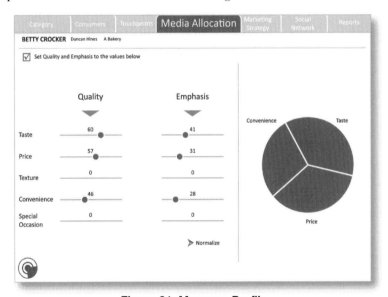

Figure 31: Message Profile

In the final piece of our model, we will define the timing of the different marketing messages and the GRP investment across these touchpoints. We assume the major competitors, Betty Crocker and Duncan Hines, invest in the lower cost channels (e.g., website, digital) and the critical marketing piece (the retail experience) throughout the year, but focus their investment for advertising and CRM direct around important holidays, such as Easter, the Fourth of July, and the late October through December holiday season.

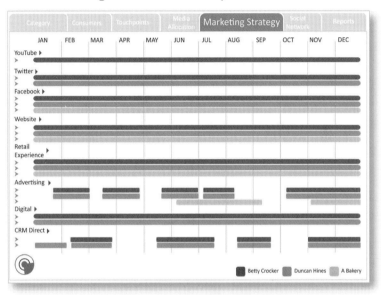

Figure 32 : Media Calendar

Now that we have built the model, we can run the simulation to compare five major areas of the model: sales, brand equity, message effect, return on investment, and the impact of word of mouth. In order to be confident with the results of our model, we will use the sales results of the model to compare with the sales that occurred during the time period under study. Another way that we may calibrate the model is to compare the resulting brand equity values at the end of our simulation with the results of a brand tracker conducted over the same time period as our one-year cake model simulation.

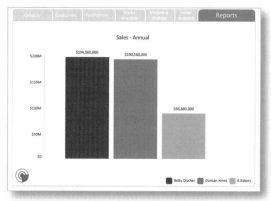

Figure 33: Sample Sales Output

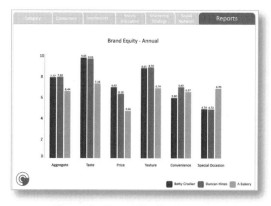

Figure 34: Brand Equity Results

The results of our simulation show that Betty Crocker is the market leader in sales (see first chart, "Sales – Annual"), but competes closely with Duncan Hines in terms of aggregate brand equity and brand equity across various aspects of the brand, including taste, price, texture, and special occasion (see second chart, "Brand Equity

— Annual"). Awareness for the regional bakery is notably lower than the major competitors (see third chart, "Product Awareness — Annual"); however, the regional bakery is perceived as superior to the major grocery-store brands with regard to its relevance for a special occasion (see second chart, "Brand Equity — Annual").

We can also analyze what contributed to the change in brand equity across the various paid, owned, and earned media touchpoints of the brands during the simulation. As the chart below shows, the paid media retail experience and advertising drove the large majority of brand equity for Betty Crocker and Duncan Hines. The regional bakery made the largest investment in advertising, which drove 66% of positive brand equity for the company.

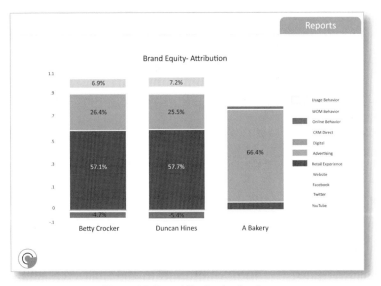

Figure 35: Brand Equity Attribution

We can also evaluate what messages resonate with the different consumer segments. As the chart below implies, communicating the good taste and texture of the three cake brands resonates with all consumer segments, but the regional bakery may want to avoid discussing their price in any of their marketing efforts given the higher cost of the regional bakery's cakes relative to the competition.

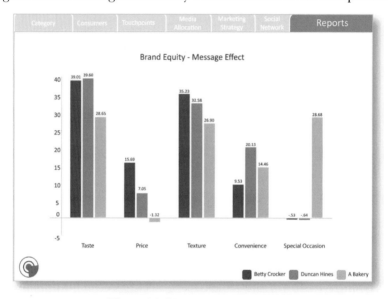

Figure 36: Message Profiles

Finally, we can also analyze the company's total return on investment, and the contribution of paid media to the company's return on investment. The regional bakery has a very high return on investment given the small percentage of their sales spent on marketing activities. All three brands generate the greatest return on investment from the retail experience and advertising.

All of these reports can be filtered by brand, attribute/driver of purchase, and consumer segment to allow for what-if analysis of one's marketing and product development strategies to assess the impact to your company and competitor reactions.

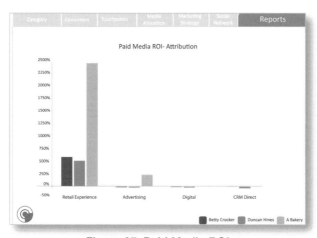

Figure 37: Paid Media ROI

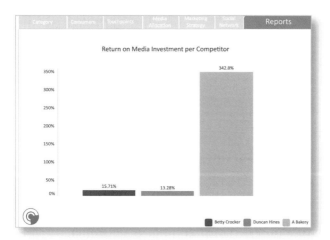

Figure 38: ROI by Competitor

As we explained at the beginning of this chapter, the real value of applying an agent-based model to inform marketing decisions and strategy is the what-if analysis and risk-free experimentation that can be achieved with this methodology. Now that we have established a baseline scenario that we are confident accurately reflects the real-world consumer and marketing environment, we can explore how changing various pieces of this framework will impact sales, brand equity, return on investment, and word-of-mouth, for our brand and our competitors.

In the first scenario we will explore, we will see how using Concentric ROI to evaluate a new marketing strategy allows for simple risk-free experimentation of a company's media allocation. In our baseline model, Betty Crocker is winning a larger share of the market with approximately $195 million in total sales, compared with annual sales of $191 million for Duncan Hines. In order to increase its share of the market, Duncan Hines may consider increasing its advertising budget for the summer months to compete more effectively with Betty Crocker. Duncan Hines will explore running an advertising campaign throughout the entire summer (May through end of August) to compare these results with a campaign for mid-May through mid-July.

This strategy proves to be successful for Duncan Hines in terms of increasing sales (from $191 million in our baseline model to $196

Figure 39: New Media Calendar

million in this scenario) and improving brand equity; however, there are implications for the company's return on investment. As a result, the company now has a negative return on investment given its high spend during the year on advertising.

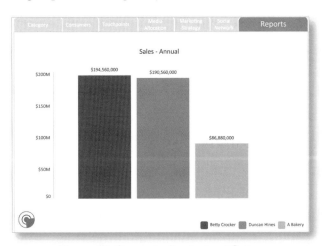

Figure 40: Scenerio Analysis of Sales

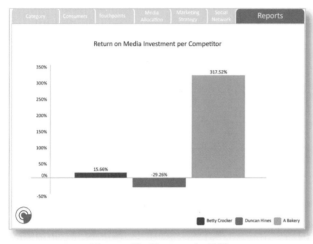

Figure 41: Change in ROI

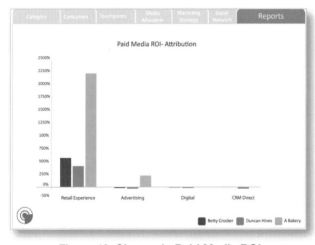

Figure 42: Change in Paid Media ROI

The regional bakery has significant challenges facing large grocery-store chains with wider distribution, greater brand recognition, and larger marketing budgets. In our baseline scenario, the regional bakery chose to invest 95% of its marketing budget in advertising, with an emphasis in the campaign on the value of the bakery for meeting the needs of a special occasion, and the superior taste, texture, and convenience of purchasing cakes at their store.

Another messaging strategy for the regional bakery may be to strictly promote the company's differentiating feature, the breadth of cakes available for a special occasion, in their advertising campaign running through the summer and the winter holiday season. We can experiment with this new strategy by altering the emphasis of the message in the "Media Allocation" section of the model.

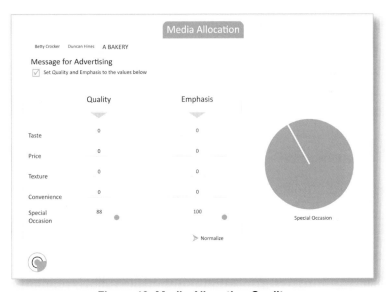

Figure 43: Media Allocation Quality

After making this change, we can rerun the simulation to observe the results, which suggest that narrowing the message of the advertising campaign is not an effective strategy in terms of sales growth or growing brand equity. In fact, as the second chart shows, brand equity declines for the regional bakery in this scenario, with the exception of brand equity for the regional bakery around relevance for a special occasion.

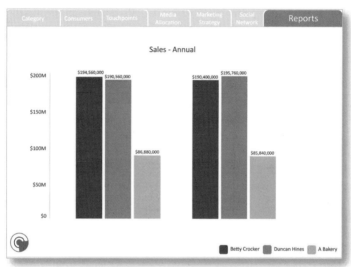

Figure 44: Sales Forecast for New Message

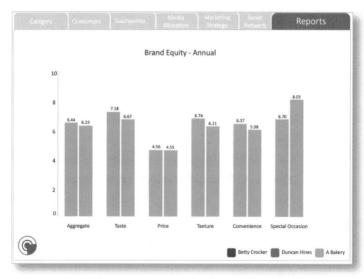

Figure 45: Brand Equity Forecast for New Message

Another valuable use of agent-based modeling is to explore the impact of new product offerings or service changes before launch. The regional bakery has advantages over store-bought cake mixes in that with a smaller operation they have the flexibility to design cakes for a variety of occasions, to meet the diverse needs of their clientele. However, the regional bakery may seek to further differentiate their product offering from grocery-store brands, by highlighting the wide selection of cakes, fillings, frostings, and garnish choices that consumers can choose from.

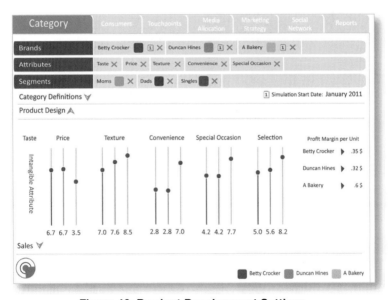

Figure 46: Product Development Settings

To examine how this product offering change may impact their business, we can simply add an attribute called "Selection" to the model. We will score how the regional bakery currently compares to Betty Crocker and Duncan Hines with regard to cake selection, and we will populate the consumer panel in the model with data on how important "Selection" is to each consumer segment, and consumers' perceptions of the three brands on this attribute.

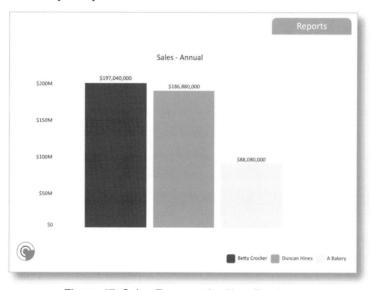

Figure 47: Sales Forecast for New Product

We can re run the simulation with this data to evaluate the potential benefit to the regional bakery of expanding their selection. Assuming the regional bakery dedicates some of their communication in their advertising to their wide selection of cakes, we can see that implementing this new strategy results in higher sales for the company. Identifying the correct communication strategy is key though, because overemphasizing the bakery's wide selection and value for a special occasion (see chart, "Message for Advertising"), and failing to communicate the regional bakery's great-tasting cakes, good prices, and convenience results in declining sales as shown below.

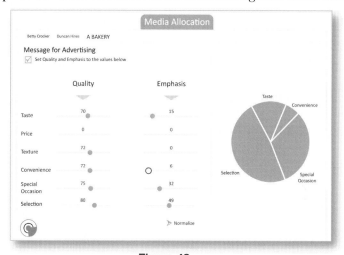

Figure 48:
Message Profile- Advertising

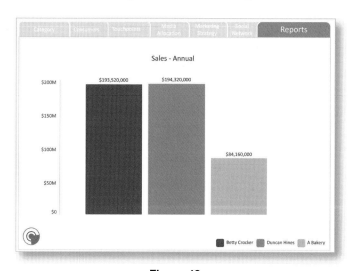

Figure 49:
Sales Forecast for Message Changes

The regional bakery can now experiment with the emphasis of their messaging to see what level of emphasis on the brand attributes (i.e., taste, price, texture, convenience, special occasion, selection) yields the desired results in terms of sales, brand equity, word of mouth, and return on investment. Our analysis suggests that the following communication strategy for the retail experience and advertising delivers the highest annual sales ($90 million) for the company.

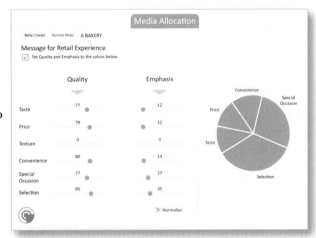

Figure 50: Optional Messaging – Retail

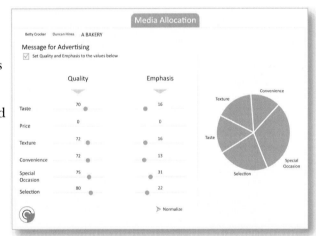

Figure 51: Optional Messaging – Advertising

Concentric ROI also allows the user to explore the value of often difficult-to-measure media. Consider a scenario where the regional bakery decides to run a Groupon promotion to drive brand awareness and sales. Measuring the impact of this new touchpoint is relatively simple to simulate with a few data inputs. We can simply add a new touchpoint to the paid media touchpoint section of the model, specify the cost of the touchpoint, and define the potential impact and reach of this touchpoint with econometric data or judgment.

We will also input the timing of the campaign and define the quality and emphasis of the Groupon promotion in the model.

Figure 52: Touchpoint Profiles

Running this new scenario shows that for the regional bakery, although the Groupon promotion raised brand awareness (from 78% in our baseline scenario to over 80% in this scenario), the new promotion did not drive higher sales or brand equity.

Figure 53: Media Calendar Example

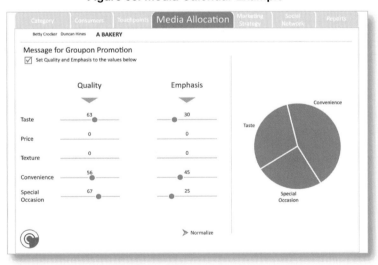

Figure 54: Profile for Groupon Ad

Testing and optimizing a company's marketing mix is also possible using Concentric ROI. For example, Betty Crocker may wish to evaluate the effects of moving some of their advertising dollars to the retail experience to evaluate the effects on sales, brand equity, and return on investment for the company as well as for their competitors. In the baseline scenario, Betty Crocker has chosen to place 71% of their marketing budget into advertising, 11% into the retail experience, and the remainder in CRM direct and digital. If

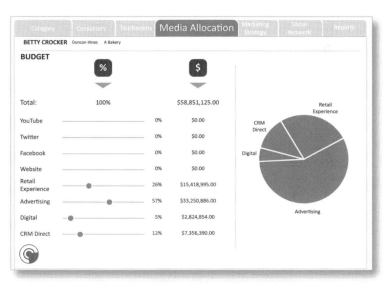

Figure 55: Optimal Allocation Spend

Betty Crocker reallocates their spend to have a greater presence in the retail experience (see the media allocation below), annual sales increase for Betty Crocker and decline for the competing brands.

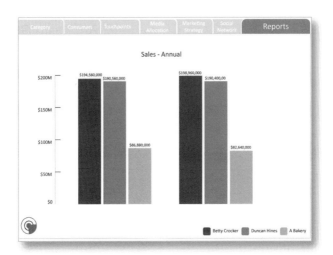

Figure 56: Forecasted Sales for New Media Allocation

Furthermore, Betty Crocker increases their brand equity on an aggregate basis and for the drivers of purchase, taste and texture. Betty Crocker's return on investment also increases in this second scenario.

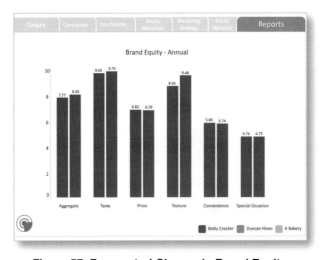

Figure 57: Forecasted Change in Brand Equity

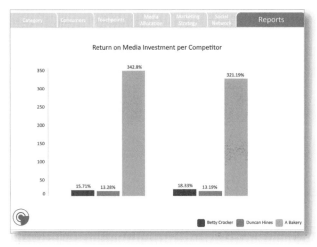

Figure 58: ROI by Competition

Betty Crocker can optimize their marketing mix through this method of redistributing the marketing spend and running the simulation to compare the results. If we experiment with a marketing mix of 53% to advertising, 24% retail experience, and 17% CRM direct, we see sales for Betty Crocker increase further, to $204 million at the expense of Duncan Hines and the regional bakery.

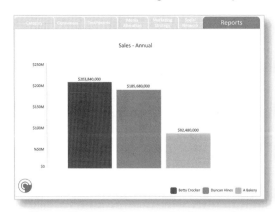

Figure 59: Sales Forecast by Competitor

Despite this improvement, Betty Crocker still has a negative return on investment from advertising, digital, and CRM direct, which may also be an important metric to the company that can be explored with further refinement of the media allocation. Within a social network we know that certain individuals are more influential than others when it comes to disseminating information and impacting the purchasing decisions of their friends and

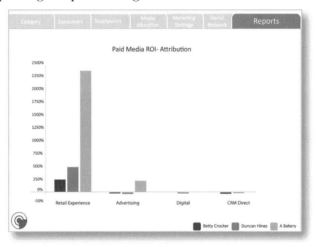

Figure 60: Media ROI

acquaintances. In social network theory these individuals are referred to as hubs, because they have a large number of social connections, and thus have significant influence on others around them. Through agent-based modeling with Concentric ROI, we can specify which consumer segments exert greater influence on consumers like them, and across different segments, and by altering these assumptions, we can analyze the impact on sales and other metrics in our model.

In our baseline model, we made an assumption that Moms typically have more influence over other Moms compared with their influence on Dads and Singles. However, if we gather new data that suggests Moms also have a high degree of influence on Singles, we can incorporate this data and observe the results.

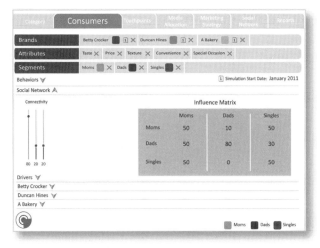

Figure 61: Social Network Influences

In changing our assumptions around consumers' level of influence, we can see that Moms' influence over the Singles segment is important, particularly for Duncan Hines. In the second scenario, greater word of mouth between Moms and Singles drove an increase in sales of approximately $10 million for Duncan Hines. Moms represent a larger proportion of the total market, and they also do more of the purchasing in our model. Greater word of mouth between Moms and Singles drove higher awareness for Singles with respect to the Duncan Hines brand, which led to higher brand perceptions for Duncan Hines around attributes that are important to Moms and Singles (see the change in product awareness for the Singles segment in the chart below).

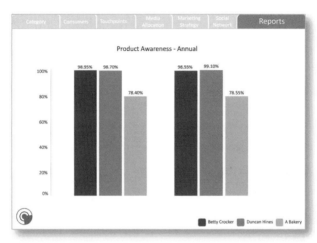

Figure 62: Product Awareness Forecast for Social Network Changes

Consumers' likelihood to engage in certain behaviors, such as discussing the brands, posting information online, or reading about cakes on online blogs or other social media, has important implications for marketers. In our baseline model, we made the assumption that Moms are more likely talk to other Moms, Dads, or Singles than other segments. We also assumed that reading about cakes and posting information online is generally low among all three segments. If we learn that Singles are actually engaging in a lot of online posting on Facebook to swap cake decorating ideas and other information, we can raise this input in the model and observe the results.

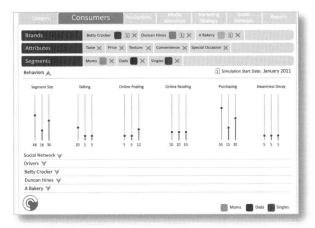

Figure 63: Earned Media Behaviors

Making this observation and reflecting the change in our model has implications for Duncan Hines and its competitors. Because Singles have influence over other Singles and are a relatively well-connected segment, the greater degree of posting leads to changes in sales for all three brands, with positive results for Betty Crocker and Duncan Hines.

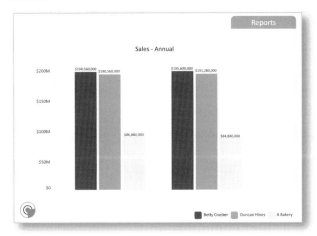

Figure 64: Sales Results for New Earned Media Behaviors

FINAL THOUGHTS: AGENT-BASED MODELING AND COMPETITION

When you implement a new marketing initiative, several things may happen. First, customers will receive new information about your product, which may cause them to update their perceptions and awareness of your product. Second, some customers may speak about your campaign or your product with others, which may cause information about your product to further spread around the social network (including to people not reached by your actual media campaign). Third, for the customers who are affected by the campaign or others in the network and actually purchase your product, this means they will experience the product, which will cause them to update their perceptions of the product in accordance with the product reality. Fourth, those who experience the product will then possibly share the information from that experience with others in their social network.

Fifth, your competition will observe this campaign and they will react.

Before agent-based modeling, there was simply no way to think these things through. We outlined five key marketing principles in the Competition paragraph above. Those five principles and the scenario described here build from game theory and are scaled up to agent-based models. Game theory is a way of studying strategic interactions between agents: consider a scenario where my best move depends on your best move, which depends on my best move. We can use mathematics to delineate each actor's best move under different levels of knowledge about the opponent, situation, or payoffs.

ABMs can help us analyze the same scenarios over many agents and many interactions. Even the most advanced game theorists cannot solve many games with a large number of actors or interactions (except when they are infinite, at which point things actually get easier). The mathematics simply become intractable. Computational capabilities mean we can now solve many more of these strategic problems, and ABMs are an ideal way to do so.

Ultimately, you know better than anyone who your competitors are, and you know where their strengths lay relative to yours, both in their products and their marketing campaigns. You are the expert, and all your knowledge and experience is readily translated into an agent-based model.

You can do this in a couple of different ways. First, if you know a lot about the competitors' likely campaigns, you can build them right in. Second, if you are not terribly sure, but have a good guess, you can make reasoned assumptions about their possible actions and explore outcomes based on those. Third, if you want to see how sensitive your campaign is to a wide range of reactions by competitors, you can sweep the probability space of outcomes and find out.

By robustness we mean something like fragility or sensitivity. A robust campaign is one whose effectiveness is not a function of what other companies do. A less robust campaign is one that only works under conditions when competitors take actions of a particular variety. A non-robust campaign is one that only works if competitors do almost nothing.

If the risk that competitors will react is low, then perhaps the non-robust but powerful message is the way to go. If you have very active competitors, you might prefer a safer route.

Of course, there's also the possibility that there exists a media campaign that is both robust and tremendously powerful and persuasive.

With a little creativity and boldness, agent-based modeling can help you find that perfect campaign — and, yes, you can even test that campaign before you roll it out.

Again, it comes back to that elusive, magical, thrilling, and slippery beast: creativity.

IN THE END

Agent-based modeling is an underused tool for making sense of complex phenomena. As we've described in this chapter, both the act of building an ABM and the analysis of the output of the model are instructive. ABMs are not substitutes for statistical modeling. They are complementary — and they often include insights gained from statistical modeling. Just because you get a new tool does not necessarily mean you no longer need the older ones.

We're going to end on an even more cautious note. ABMs are not a panacea. They help you explore, analyze, and test ideas. Calibration can let you test your assumptions against sales results. Are your mental models about the world right?

ABMs are a really exciting tool. But what matters most is what has always mattered — rigor, facts, and judgment. When the user is no longer responsible for the outcome, the model ceases to be meaningful.

We are not offering being right; we're offering the ability to understand changes in scenarios. This means being able to make better decisions that lead to better results — and the better your information, the better your results. At the end of the day, we're only as good as our assumptions, and so your expertise and research teams are extremely valuable.

We believe that because many of the ABMs you will use will call for expertise, this should have the additional benefit of improving how you develop solutions to your problems. Perhaps you will come up with better resource allocation or a more creative workflow in order to make your ABM even better. We would love it.

Read Further

Bikhchandani, S., D. Hirschleifer, and I. Welch. 1992. *A Theory of Fads, Fashions, Custom, and Cultural Change as Information Cascades.* The Journal of Political Economy 100(5), 992-1026.

McKenna, Edward. 2004. *Econometrics.* New London, CT: Connecticut College, course manual.

Miller, John C. and Scott E. Page. 2007. *Complex Adaptive Systems: An Introduction to Computational Models of Social Life.* Princeton: Princeton University Press.

Mitchell, Melanie. 2009. *Complexity: A Guided Tour.* Oxford: Oxford University Press.

Page, Scott E. 1999. *Computational Models from A to Z.* Complexity 5(1): 35-41.

Page, Scott E. 2008. *The Difference: How the Power of Diversity Creates Better Schools, Companies, and Communities.* Princeton, NJ: Princeton University Press.

Schelling, Thomas C. 1971. *Dynamic Models of Segregation.* Journal of Mathematical Sociology 1:143-186.

CONCLUSION

Just as we outlined the change from the individual to the system in Part One, we endeavor now to outline the changes that have occurred from the brand to the competitive environment. In doing so, we are not trying to change the types of decisions that are made but rather are trying to change the mindset with which we approach those decisions. Gone are the days when we have to wonder about what part of "my" marketing is working. We can understand now how it works and what the underlying dynamics of every decision made are.

To us the shift to understanding is an affirmation of our interconnectedness, a mindset that we believe is the only answer to the static approach to marketing that has dominated for so long. Static measurement, while important and valid, has always lacked a means for "pulling it together." With the development of agent-based modeling, we are no longer lacking of means. We can now attribute the entirety of the brand experience to cause and effect. We can understand the interplay of marketing spend, product quality, word of mouth, competitor actions, price and all other parts of the brand experience. This understanding of creativity and strategy can be expressed numerically as part of predictive modeling and analytics. This means that CEO's, CFO's, and CMO's need to enhance their working relationships.

We believe that good modeling is as much about good results as it is about good process. We hope that with this book and/or technology in your office, you will find yourself making more holistic choices, not just in terms of your product but in terms of how you spend your team's and your energy in the office. Consensus building is a big side benefit of using ABMs as part of your analytical toolkit.

For us, the mystery is no longer about whether we can capture data and develop models. The mystery is: when will marketers stop making the same decisions in the same way? Through the discussions in this book, we hope to build momentum for a more proactive and thorough understanding that will elevate the marketing craft to a more respected designation within corporations, where its practitioners have a firmer grip on its seat at the table. That is our mission. That is our passion. That is our hope.

APPENDIX

APPENDIX A: NETWORKS

For the interested reader, we provide more details on network analysis. Please also read the recommended books in the "Read Further" listing at the end of Chapter 3.

Randomness

We can measure networks in terms of their randomness coefficient. Let's call it p and let p = 0 to refer to networks that are totally ordered and p = 1 to refer to networks that are totally random. When p is low, the average degree of separation and the clustering coefficient both tend to be high.

Small World

Although you may have heard of small world networks, we are going to tell you specifically what they mean (and don't mean), and why they matter.

A "small world" network refers to a network topology where each node has many nearby connections and a few long distance ones. This holds easily in most of social life: you have close friends, family, or coworkers you interact with regularly. You also know many people with whom you don't interact on a regular basis.

At this juncture, you might be thinking: wait! Because of Facebook and email I am in touch with many people far away. Your antiquated definition is meaningless! Actually, your Facebook network is probably also a small world one, only this time your connections are not measured by geographical distance; rather, they are measured by frequency of communication. You have a handful of Facebook friends with whom you interact regularly, and many with whom you rarely connect.

Small world networks are especially relevant to marketing because they describe two phenomena: first, most people in a social network are actually not directly connected. Second, messages can still travel between people in a social network, even if they are not connected directly to one another, through very few steps.

Distribution

How do you know if a network is a small world variation or another form of a social network? We can tell by eyeballing the picture of the network, but we'd like to be able to know for sure. One way we can be specific about the type of network with which we are working is to ask: how are the connections distributed? This is a way of measuring not just overall connectivity, but how each actor is connected to others. A uniform distribution would mean that everyone has the same number of ties. A normal distribution means that most people have an average number of ties, while some have very few and some have very many. One of the most interesting distributions is a scale-free distribution, or a power law distribution.

Small world networks are an example of a power law or scale-free distributed network. There are a lot of really interesting things you can do and measure about scale-free networks, but we won't address anywhere close to all of them here (see Read Further at the end of this appendix for more). The thing to know for now about power law distributed networks is that they refer to networks where the vast majority of people have a small-to-average number of connections and a few people have a LOT of connections.

It's called a power law distribution because the power law itself refers to any population where most people have a few of something and a handful has much more of it. The term "scale-free" comes from the phenomenon where you can zoom in or out in a network or some other power law distributed body and still observe a power law. If you take a small world network, you can zoom way in and see that it is still a small world network. At levels that take in the whole network or at levels that take in just a handful of clusters, the power law still holds. If you're thinking that sounds basically insane and amazing, you're following along perfectly.

Connectivity

In addition to the distribution of connections, we can think about how many ties each individual has. Again, in most social circles, some people have very few ties, but the vast majority of us have a number of about 100 people with whom we interact remotely regularly. And, a few of us have tons and tons of friends. We all know that guy. This is again an example of a power law distribution, and the node that has a lot more connections than most nodes is called a hub. (The use of this word in airline routes is not a coincidence.)

But here we're talking specifically about connection counts, not just distribution. You can have a power law distributed network that shows high connectivity or low connectivity.

If most people have a number of connections slightly lower than the average number, and a few people have tons of connections, does this mean that if you wanted to send a message to the most people with the least effort, you should target the people with the most connections?

Not necessarily. It's actually not just about who is connected to the most people. It also matters what type of people are involved, and it matters what they're talking about. We'll get to that in just a minute.

APPENDIX B: MODELING

Just as we cannot consider all cakes when we buy, we cannot consider everything when we model a marketing environment. To reduce our marketing campaigns to a set of variables, let's take a step back and look at the ways in which scientific models are created across many fields.

One way to build a model is to use deduction: To look at a number of data points about the real world and work backwards to find a general mathematical representation that will explain the behavior of the real world behavior with some degree of precision. Much of scientific progress has occurred in this way since the period of Enlightenment. Mostly due to the philosophy of Francis Bacon, often called the Father of the Scientific Method, prevailing wisdom regarding research held that hypotheses should be developed by unprejudiced observation of nature. To the extent that marketing research today can be said to aim at finding models to explain the behavior of societies, most current research would be characterized as deductive, as marketers and analysts pour over various data sources and attempt (mostly through regression techniques or Bayesian models) to find equations that represent the behavior of the system they are analyzing. Media mix models, for example, find correlations among data sets about spend and response (whether purchase or perception or awareness) in order to optimize the marketing spend allocation.

The other way to build models is to use induction: to build a model based on intuition, logic, or various reasoning and work forward in refining that model until accurate prediction is achieved. Among the most dramatic examples of inductive reasoning is Albert Einstein's Theory of Special Relativity, for which he famously imagined riding on a beam of light. Without poring over any astronomical data, and at the reported age of 16, Einstein did a thought experiment that uncovered gaps in the prevailing physics wisdom of the time. Without inferring that our thinking is either as profound or as sophisticated as that of the leading theoretical physicists of our time, we undertake an inductive approach to modeling. This approach is based on three principles: simplicity, validity, and usefulness.

Simplicity, Validity, and Usefulness

To borrow from Einstein's intellect one more time, he said "a model should be as simple as possible, but no simpler." Besides the aesthetic value of a simple model, aiming for simplicity in models is based on three observations. First, it takes only very simple rules to produce highly complex behavior. For example, the physicist and computer scientist Stephen Wolfram spent decades analyzing a particular set of models called cellular automata, as a new approach to recreate naturally occurring complex systems. Without going into the details of cellular automata, Wolfram's finding is that models based on only a handful of rules produce extraordinary complexity that mimics the behavior of markets, formation of patterns in nature, and even emergence of life. In Wolfram's words: "One might think that if one were to increase the complexity of the rules, then the behavior one would get would also become increasingly more complex." Studies show that as a general rule, once a threshold for complex behavior has been reached, adding additional complexity to the underlying rules does not lead to any perceptible increase at all in the overall complexity of the behavior produced.

The second rationale for selecting variables or rules you include in a model is that the simpler a model is, the more likely it is that it will be general across various environments and situations. When modeling individuals in a marketing context, our assumption is that awareness, drivers, and perceptions apply to any marketing environment where people choose among a set of alternatives that are defined through a set of attributes. The situations that the model generalizes can vary from the purchase of facial tissue to political elections, the sale of equipment, and, of course, decisions regarding cakes.

The third rationale for simplicity is the most practical one: simpler models allow us to find what is responsible for overall behavior more easily. If there are fewer variables and features of the system, it is less likely that we will be led astray in our understanding of the results of the model. This idea is familiar to statisticians who regularly eliminate variables with low statistical significance in order to prune the model until all variables have an effect on the outcomes of the system.

Simplicity by itself is not enough to make a good model, as the model is only as good as the extent to which it replicates the real world. To validate decisions regarding modeling choices we have made, we must check whether our assumptions and their predicted results are accurate. Let's start with a few words on our choice of assumptions. One influential empirical analysis of the way people make decisions was performed by psychologist John W. Payne and described in his book *The Adaptive Decision-Maker.* Payne performed a series of experiments in which he asked respondents to choose from fictional alternatives of houses to buy. In setting up the experiment, Payne arranged different offerings of houses as a matrix of envelopes taped to a wall in such a way that each column of envelopes represented a house that could be chosen and each row was an attribute (e.g., price, square feet, number of rooms, etc.). Inside the envelopes were the actual values of the attributes. In order for respondents to find out how a particular house fared on any attribute, the respondents had to open the envelope and read the value. The reason Payne set up the experiment this way was to uncover the process with which people go about selecting from various alternatives.

The utility maximizing model of choice would require that each respondent open all envelopes for the first alternative, score the utility of that alternative, repeat the process until all alternatives were scored, and finally choose the alternative with the highest utility. Respondents did nothing of the sort. Instead, they usually opened envelopes that were located in rows that corresponded to the attribute they found most important. Price-conscious respondents checked the prices of all alternatives first, while room-conscious respondents checked the number of rooms available for each alternative. Then, respondents eliminated some alternatives that they found unsatisfactory for the most important attribute and moved on to the next important attribute while only opening envelopes for the alternatives remaining. By filtering the information, most of the respondents converged quickly to a choice without opening the majority of the envelopes on the board. Payne's experiments showed that people were using filtering as a heuristic way to maximize the value of alternatives on important attributes while minimizing the computational effort required to make the decision.

Payne's result was theoretically anticipated a decade before by two pioneers of behavioral economics, both of whom eventually earned Nobel Prizes for their work, Kahneman and Tversky. As an alternative process to the utility maximization model, Kahneman and Tversky proposed a decision-making model called elimination by aspects (EBA), which mathematically represents the filtering mechanism that Payne's respondents actually used.

The EBA model is different from the utility maximization model in three fundamental ways that generally differentiate rationally bounded models from those of traditional economic theory. First, EBA does not require decision makers to use all of the available information. Decision-makers stop their search for a good alternative once they have found one that satisfies their most important needs. Second, the model of decision-making is probabilistic: the same decision-maker will sometimes choose one alternative over another even when nothing about the decision-making environment changes. Third, choices depend on the sequence with which decision-makers evaluate alternatives. If by chance a decision-maker has stumbled upon a "good" alternative, she may choose that alternative, without checking if the next one coming is actually better.

Comparing the two models, EBA and utility maximization, Kahneman, Tversky, and Payne uncovered that when the alternatives and attributes are few, the two decision-making models are identical in their predictions. However, for more complicated decisions that involve large numbers of alternatives and many attributes that define them, people systematically deviate from the predictions of the standard economic theories of rational choice and engage in heuristic choice processes, which lead to choices that are often not optimal.

Replicating this irrational and suboptimal decision process is where an agent-based model is perfectly suited to help. Given that the properties of the mind remain identical for each agent, all that it takes to change the decision-making process of an agent is to assign it a different set of rules. In fact, we could even make meta-rules that govern under which conditions certain agents will use one decision-making process over another, using empirical evidence like the one offered by Payne. For example, we could have a rule specifying that people will use utility maximization when they are aware of three alternatives or less but they will use EBA for any larger choice set. Furthermore, given that agent-based modeling allows us to create heterogeneous populations, we could have two sub-populations or segments: more rational agents as a proxy for people who are more involved in the decision process (whose threshold of using utility maximization is much higher than three alternatives), and less rational agents as a proxy for people who spend less effort in deciding.

The mind model is still grounded in simple rules. Its validity could be derived by systematically calibrating the thresholds and the decision-making processes chosen until the behavior of the agent-based model mimics the experimental or the real world data.

Finally, the model would be useful to the extent that a decision-maker could experiment with different choice environments (the number of products that are displayed on a shelf or on a website and the number of attributes that are shown to the consumer) and analyze which type of decision-makers are likely to buy which product. This approach follows our simple, valid, useful philosophy.

About the Authors

Greg Silverman is an innovator and entrepreneur who has worked in the Marketing Analytics field for over 15 years. Previously he was the Global Managing Director of Interbrand's Analytics Practice and is currently the CEO of Concentric, a predictive marketing software company

Dejan Duzevik is a pioneer in Agent-Based Modeling (ABM), always seeking better explanations of the complexity of social dynamics and decision-making. He is currently the CTO of Concentric, where he helps people and companies around the world in their pursuits for better analytics, strategy, and knowledge.

Andrea Jones-Rooy's life goal is to discover how patterns in the spread of information can improve the survival rates of groups, companies, and countries. She has a Ph.D. in Political Science and Complex Systems from the University of Michigan, Ann Arbor, and is a postdoctoral fellow in Social and Decision Sciences at Carnegie Mellon University.

INDEX